GARDENING IS FO

HUMAN HORIZONS SERIES

GARDENING IS FOR EVERYONE

A Week-by-Week Guide for People with Handicaps

AUDREY CLOET & CHRIS UNDERHILL

Illustrated by Sue Fairhurst

With a Foreword by Alan Gemmell

A CONDOR BOOK
SOUVENIR PRESS (E & A) LTD

Foreword

In a long career in which gardening has played an increasingly dominant part I have read many gardening books, but never one quite like this. It is the first I have come across which attempts to present gardening as a means of helping the handicapped, irrespective of whether the disability is physical or mental, to achieve results in jobs that they can carry out alone or in small groups.

In such work it is essential that results should be forthcoming in order to instil or sustain a feeling of confidence in one's abilities. Work with living things such as plants makes it dreadfully easy to set up nice little exercises which just don't work. This book avoids that pitfall, for it lays out in a very basic, straightforward style, a one-year course in practical gardening.

I know that many people who help and care for the handicapped have been brought up in cities where gardening is regarded as something done in the country or suburbia. Through no fault of their own they may lack the instinctive feel and confidence for doing the right things with plants. What was needed, therefore, was a text describing in simple terms appropriate jobs and even experiments that could be carried out with the minimum of equipment by almost anyone. (I say *almost* anyone simply to cover myself, for I am constantly amazed by the most extraordinary degree of skill and success achieved by even the most severely handicapped.)

This is such a book. After a very thoughtful introduction to the technicalities of running a practical course in gardening, the major part is devoted to a suggested week-by-week series of practical classes, each described in considerable detail ranging from making sure you have an old newspaper or some eggshells handy, to simple instructions for mixing compost and sowing seeds. Slavishly followed, each task will work, for they have mostly been tested on handicapped groups, but the good and imaginative teacher will quickly see modifications and extensions of the techniques and materials described. In some cases modifications could easily come from the group itself.

When I start to dwell on the pleasure I get from gardening a number of thoughts come immediately to mind. For example, the mere fact that things grow and change is interesting, in that the most successful plants are those that adapt to their environment. In this way things progress. Again, there is the idea that if one crop of seeds fails one can always try again, maybe using slightly different timings or methods. Nothing is final and finished.

Yet another thought is very basic to me. In planting, watering, feeding and generally caring for the plant I get a sense of having personally created it. I feel I have done something positive, of which I can be proud, and which if I am lucky may be really beautiful.

Such thoughts may seem superficial, but they are nonetheless real and add another dimension to the purely physical pleasures one gets from work and manipulation. All this is surely part of the horticultural therapy.

The practical nature of this book is summed up in the appendices which list books, addresses, places to visit, tool and seed suppliers and many other useful things.

I can only commend the skill shown by the writers in devising such a workable set of basic gardening jobs and in presenting them in clear and above all practical terms.

Alan R. Gemmell
May 1982

Contents

PART TWO: Gardening Recipes

Acknowledgements

This book is based on the experience we have gained through our work with the Society for Horticultural Therapy, and we should like to thank the many people who have shared their ideas, discussed their problems and written to tell us about their experiences.

Our thanks to all the staff of HT who have given advice and encouragement, and especially to Judi, Tracy and Madeline for typing the manuscript in a year which was already hectic.

We should also like to thank Sue Fairhurst for her beautiful drawings, our dear friend Dolly Robertson for consenting to appear on the cover, and also the members of the Bath Stroke Club for trying out some of the 'recipes'.

Most of all, our thanks to the Joseph Rowntree Memorial Trust for funding the work which went into the book, and for their sponsorship of Horticultural Therapy in the community.

A.C.
C.U.
Horticultural Therapy,
Goulds Ground, Vallis Way,
Frome, Somerset BA11 3DW

"Healing is a matter of time; it is also sometimes a matter of opportunity".

Hippocrates

Part One

1 Aims

It would be foolish to make extravagant claims for gardening as a cure-all, but as an activity which is both rewarding and extraordinarily adaptable in its application, it is probably the most widely used therapeutic medium. Contact with the world of plants is a vital part of human experience, and to be able to participate in some form of gardening brings real pleasure to many people. People of all ages and with widely differing interests and abilities enjoy growing all kinds of things, and handicapped people are no exception. Like everyone else, they feel a sense of achievement when seeds sprout and plants flourish, and there are no barriers between gardeners. Plants, after all, make no differentiation – they simply respond to care and attention.

Handicapped people have fewer opportunities than others of choosing their environment and adapting it, but gardening is one way in which they can express personal tastes and bring beauty into their surroundings. Most disabled people live at home, and the gardening they do is most likely to be on a small scale – on a windowsill, a balcony, or in a small garden. We especially wanted to write a book which would help people to make the most of their surroundings and to use every available space, from a bedside locker to a back garden, for growing something to enjoy. We have planned a programme of activities suitable for most age-groups, needing a minimum amount of space and equipment and assuming no previous horticultural knowledge. If it is used as a basis for a regular session with a group, it will take about an hour once a week. The guide-lines in choosing the programme were that topics should arouse interest, lead to the acquisition of new skills, and give a sense of achievement by producing satisfying and successful results.

The activities are varied, and designed to give some

experience of basic gardening techniques such as seed-sowing, taking cuttings, transplanting and caring for plants. Beginners like to have 'instant' gardening, so some topics have been chosen for their fun appeal and quick results. Even experienced gardeners are intrigued by watching the development of roots and shoots at close quarters, so a few water-culture items have been included for observation. Some plants offer hobby possibilities and a number of topics have been chosen as 'starters' for potential enthusiasts. Germinating pips and stones, for instance, may lead to bonsai-growing; taking leaf-cuttings from African violets could be the start of a flourishing light-garden.

Things to eat or to give away are always satisfying. This is not a guide to serious vegetable gardening, so a few things particularly suitable for container growing have been selected. Making use of flowers and seed-heads for craft work can give a great deal of pleasure, and looking for interesting material leads to increased awareness of both wild and cultivated plants.

This is not 'easy gardening' – the 'no-work' garden is not necessarily what a disabled person requires – but no-one wants to do things the hard way deliberately, so methods of simplifying work and reducing the effort required are always welcome. Our aim is to make gardening enjoyable and to enable people to do more of it, not less.

2 Notes for Helpers

AN HOUR A WEEK

In planning a weekly session with a group, a regular pattern is necessary to maintain continuity. The topics in this book can each be covered in a session of an hour, which is about the maximum time for keeping the interest of a group. Remember that it takes time for a group to assemble and also clean up at the end, so keep a discreet eye on the time.

Some groups of course, are slower than others in assembling and settling down, and the gardening activity may be part of an afternoon session which includes serving tea at a specific time. Even in a leisured atmosphere, it is wise to keep to a schedule. A short, well structured session is better than one in which some members of the group lose interest, or one which ends in a scramble to clean up. Cleaning up is an essential part of the activity – so plan enough time towards the end of the session for this, and do not land yourself with a mammoth task alone afterwards.

The programme is arranged in small 'bites' – this is the most effective way of learning new techniques. Aim for maximum achievement by trying to ensure success in every possible way. Give clear instructions and discreetly check on each stage to avoid mistakes (e.g. bulbs planted upside down), tactfully point out any error and on no account be tempted to correct it yourself. Make aftercare instructions very plain and in succeeding weeks give reminders. It may be a good idea to write out directions about aftercare and give each member of the group a copy – this could make valuable writing practice for those who need it, or form part of the scrap-book or diaries mentioned in the Planning Session (page 62).

Where the members of the group are 'living in', either in residential accommodation or in hospital, it is important to maintain a good relationship with those in charge. Inform them of your plans, get to know the do's and don'ts of the establishment and fit in with routine practices. Your proposed session may have to fit into a pattern of other activities and it is important to gain the confidence of busy staff; in return you will find a willingness to co-operate over practical arrangements, plant sales, outings and displaying the decorations made by the group. Day to day help may be needed to maintain plant-care between sessions – this is much easier if you have the understanding and goodwill of the staff. Making a few extra gifts in a craft session to give to the staff involved would be a nice gesture.

Do remember to leave a few minutes to announce the topic planned for next week's session, and ask for any help needed in bringing materials.

LOOKING AHEAD

Look ahead to future programmes, to see whether preparation is needed, or materials need to be collected or bought. It is especially valuable to ask for help from the group in collecting every-day objects like yoghurt pots, jam jars, etc., and in bringing material for cuttings. This encourages involvement and co-operation as well as anticipation of the next meeting. But avoid saying something like, "Each person must bring two plastic cups". Just "Next week we will be needing. . . ." will usually produce more than enough, without creating undue pressure on the less capable members of the group. But always safeguard against being short of materials for the group by bringing some along yourself.

People may have missed out – through illness or late joining of the group perhaps – and not have rooted cuttings or seedlings to transplant. Be prepared for this by growing some at home and taking them along to the session. This will also take care of the possible failures.

PLANT MATERIAL

You need some plants to provide cuttings: these are the 'stock' plants which should be healthy and pest free. They could be part of the permanent planting in the garden – shrubs and ivies for instance – or form part of the display of indoor plants which are used for decoration. You may have to bring the plants from home or ask your friends to help by donating cuttings. Several plants of each kind may be needed to supply enough cuttings for a whole group.

To give the best chance of success, the basic material to choose should ideally have most of the following qualities:
  - easy to grow by an inexperienced gardener
  - not too fussy about growing conditions
  - tough enough to handle without breaking easily
  - easily grown from seed, or simple to propagate by taking cuttings
  - relatively free from pests and diseases.

SOME USEFUL PLANT MATERIAL

Flowering plants
Begonia semperflorens (wax begonia)
Beloperone (Shrimp Plant)
Fuchsia
Impatiens (Busy Lizzie)
Pelargonium (Geranium)
Saintpaulia (African Violet)

Foliage plants
Coleus
Chlorophytum (Spider Plant)
Cissus antarctica (Kangaroo Vine)
Hedera (Ivy)
Iresine (Blood Leaf)
Peperomia
Philodendron scandens (Sweetheart Plant)
Pilea (Aluminium Plant)
Plectranthus (Swedish Ivy)
Sanseveria (Mother-in-law's Tongue)
Saxifraga sarmentosa (Mother of Thousands)
Tradescantia (including Setcreasea, Zebrina)

Succulents
Bryophyllum (Good Luck Plant)
Crassula (Jade Plant)
Echeveria
Sedum (Jelly Bean Plant, etc.)
Sempervivum (Houseleek, etc.)
Senecio (String of Beads Plant)

A PRACTICE RUN
If the technique is unfamiliar to you, try out the 'recipe' beforehand. Being well prepared is the secret of running a successful group, and of creating a relaxed atmosphere without anxiety or haste.

Knowing your group, can you foresee any problems? A practice run will enable you to judge what difficulties your group might meet, and to decide on what method to use. It is sometimes stimulating to meet a challenge. It is a matter of judgement whether tough things will prove discouraging, or give a greater feeling of achievement. You may have some ideas of your own that are particularly appropriate. (If you do, please write in to The Society for Horticultural Therapy – bright ideas for solving problems are always welcome!)

YOUR GARDENING GROUP

Choosing a name for the group – even if this arises casually and not as a deliberate naming session – gives identity to the group, and a special feeling about the weekly session.

Encourage the participants to use the sessions as a stimulus for other activities – nature study, bird watching, visiting gardens open to the public, arranging trips to botanical gardens, planning for films and visiting speakers on gardening topics, flower arranging demonstrations and so on. Some members of a group will probably already have a special interest in one of these topics, and enjoy sharing their enthusiasm with the others.

FOR EXAMPLE?

With some of the craft topics you may feel that it is useful to take along your own try-out to give some idea of the end-result that you hope will be achieved. But most often it is better to leave people free to use their own talents and imagination. It is amazing how much more original work is produced when people feel free to do things in their own way.

By all means help those who are floundering, perhaps by providing step-by-step examples, but it is important to encourage the expression of personal taste wherever possible, by offering a choice of colours, flowers, etc.

In presenting a finished sample at the very beginning of the session, the stimulus of curiosity about the new materials is lost. To arrive with an intriguing assortment of things – whether it be plants, craft material, pots or pebbles – is more likely to arouse comment and the urge to participate than to be shown an example and then to be given materials to work with afterwards.

In addition, it is possible that a demonstration sample may be interpreted as 'ideal' – and therefore as a measure of failure if a similar standard is not achieved. Any efforts must be regarded as having a value, even if the results are a little clumsy. The handling of different objects, with varying shapes, sizes and textures, is a stimulus in itself and the experience is worthwhile in therapeutic terms.

PROTECTIVE MEASURES

Gardening can be messy so you need to think about some form
of protection.

Aprons to keep clothes clean

Members of the group may prefer to protect their clothing
from compost, water, sprays or glue by wearing an apron or
smock. Old shirts are good – they protect the sleeves as well.

Some means of cleaning hands after the session

There may be nearby washrooms or a sink in the room. Check
that towels are available and if not, provide paper towels. You
could use a bowl or bucket of water but if this is not practicable
at least provide pre-moistened tissues. A plastic bag of damp
paper towels and a supply of dry ones would not be too difficult
to arrange.

Plastic sheets to protect the table tops

Even if the table tops are formica covered it may be preferred
that you protect them from scratches. You can use newspaper –
this makes for swift clearing up, but it gets soggy with water,
and the print makes sleeves dirty. For some activities you may
need to spread plastic sheets or paper on the floor.

Protection for hands

People with allergies may need to protect their hands. You
could use household gloves, gardening gloves or for very fine
work, the thin disposable plastic gloves.

Bed covers

For bed patients some form of protection for the sheets is
essential. Old plastic table cloths are generally softer, slightly
textured and so less slippery than the usual plastic sheeting.

MEASUREMENTS

Although the book includes instructions about measurements
in both centimetres and inches, the instructions are not meant
to be intimidating or too precise. It is simply to answer the

question, "How far apart and how deep?", because some guidance may be needed to grow plants successfully. In practice you can translate these into more homely instructions, "As deep as your finger nail", for instance. Hands are useful measures. Stretch out your fingers on a ruler and measure the span. What is the length of your thumb from the tip of the nail to the first knuckle? Use the things you have around – you may find a measurement is more easily understood as the 'width of a label' or 'the length of a trowel'.

There are other measurements of weight or volume which can be translated into homely terms. Granular fertiliser which is applied in grams per square metre (or ounces per square yard) is simpler to measure out in egg-cups or small cans. After weighing out a sample of the required amount, try out a number of small containers and find one which will hold it, preferably exactly so that scooping out and levelling off the top will give the right measure. An automatic tea-caddy will dispense spoonfuls of powdered or granular fertiliser, and this is useful if one does not want to handle the fertiliser.

Liquid measurements are simple – there are plenty of litre and pint bottles around, always remembering never to use soft drink bottles or returnable milk bottles as containers for anything other than water. Similarly, for safety's sake be careful to avoid the use of cups or jugs.

Long measuring sticks are very useful for spacing out plants, and the required intervals can be marked with notches or round-headed screws. This is a particularly valuable aid for those who are visually handicapped. As you put the work into practice, you will find that many other ideas will occur to you.

3 Basics for Gardeners and Their Helpers

GARDEN PLANNING

The first consideration in planning a garden is accessibility. It should be easy to move around in – which means good paths and non-slip surfaces – and there should be easy access from the house.

Then one should consider the factors which will give the maximum use and pleasure from the area available. This takes into account the needs and physical ability of the gardener. Some people would like to produce the maximum display with a minimum of effort, and others look on their garden as an area which will provide a great deal of occupation and in which they will use every space intensively.

Ideally the area of maximum interest should be visible from the windows of rooms which are used frequently. Even when one is indoors it is a pleasure to see an attractive garden and to be aware of one's achievements.

Attracting wildlife to the garden can add to this 'interest from indoors'. Butterflies can be encouraged to visit the garden by carefully choosing plants which they may like (see page 202 at the end of the book). A birdbath is an attraction all the year round and food can be put out in the winter (see December, Week Four). Birds add life and interest to the garden even in the bleakest months.

Planning the sitting areas with care makes a great difference to the amount of pleasure which can be obtained. To be able to enjoy sitting in the garden, either doing jobs, chatting with friends or just relaxing, encourages one to spend more time out of doors. Choose for preference a place in the sun, sheltered from the wind or cold draughts, with some provision for shade in the hottest weather.

Remember to lay on a supply of water and make some

provision for storing tools and equipment. Keen gardeners will need to think about such things as cold frames and plunge beds, and perhaps even a small greenhouse or potting shed.

Gardens which are divided into small areas are not so discouraging to the individual disabled gardener and invite interesting planting. Where a garden is shared by a group it may not be possible to allocate individual plots, so careful planning is needed to create opportunities for personal achievement. Container growing may be one way of ensuring individual responsibility and satisfaction. With ingenuity, even a bleak concrete yard can offer a lot of planting space with growing bags, a variety of containers and hanging baskets and the use of trellis on the walls for climbing plants.

RAISED BEDS

Raised beds have often been identified with gardening for the disabled, most especially for those in wheelchairs. In fact, most gardeners would enjoy doing some work at this level. The plants gain extra impact from being raised and some small plants such as alpines are more readily appreciated. It is easy to keep well-defined areas like this free from weeds. Raised borders, terraces and wall-top planting are attractive features in good garden designs.

Making beds of various heights need not necessarily mean constructing them of brick or stone. There are all sorts of alternatives, ranging from tyres, sewer pipes and old sinks to peat blocks and railway sleepers. Some of these 'home-made' beds should always be included in the garden of a rehabilitation unit as they are the most likely to be built when the patient returns home.

Containers of many different kinds, from elegant stone urns to old dustbins, can bring growing to all kinds of levels so that gardening while sitting down – or at waist level while standing – is a practical possibility.

It is difficult, however, to design a raised bed which is comfortable to use from a wheelchair, as working sideways for any length of time is tiring – and may not be advisable. Considerable thought has been put into the design of table-like planters which allow for knee-room. The planting depth is necessarily shallow, so there is the problem of constant watering and of choosing plants which will do well in such conditions. Some raised beds have been designed which have a deep centre part and a lipped edge to allow gardeners in wheelchairs to work face-on, but these are likely to be more expensive than ordinary raised beds.

Many people find it more satisfactory to do most of the fiddly work at an ordinary table or on a tray fixed to a wheelchair. Seed trays or pots can be transferred to a bench or table for intermediate care before planting out at a more mature and less demanding stage.

Some people would rather garden at ground level, using long-handled tools if they find bending or reaching difficult, or work kneeling or even lying on the ground. Raised beds are not, therefore, a universal requirement of gardening for disabled people. If you do want to go ahead and build them, make sure that they are properly designed for the people who are to use them. Suitable edges, securely anchored hand rails, toe holes, water supply and drainage as well as the cost and aesthetic siting are all factors to be considered.

THE NEED FOR SHELTER

When trying to run an all-the-year round programme it is obvious that much of the work must be done indoors and that anything which makes it possible for work to be done under cover is a great advantage. In the winter these extra areas, such as a conservatory or greenhouse, would have to be heated to work in comfortably. In warmer months, a potting shed or polythene tunnel would give shelter from the rain.

Proportion of Indoor/Outdoor Work

If too much of the planned work is out of doors, there is the danger of having nothing to do on wet days and then an incredible rush on fine ones. One requirement of a programme with handicapped people is that it should offer a regularly enjoyable activity which is not overwhelming in its demands. To spread the work evenly it is necessary to include plenty of indoor work, some which could be done indoors or out, and only a small proportion which is essentially out of doors. The one day-a-week session may happen to fall on a succession of wet Thursdays!

Adapting the Programme

The unreliability of the weather makes it necessary to take advantage of fine days. The programme can and should be switched around to get on with outdoor jobs like preparing the soil and planting out when the weather is good. The only thing to beware of is the temptation to sow the seeds too early or to plant out tender summer plants before the frosts are over.

SHELTER FOR PLANTS

It is not necessary to have a greenhouse to grow the things in this book. A sunny windowsill is enough or better still a table in front of the window to give more growing space indoors. Greenhouses are sometimes a problem to disabled people, not only because heating is expensive, but because considerable physical effort is needed to maintain them. Without proper glasshouse hygiene, plants eventually suffer all kinds of ailments.

Out of doors it is better to use things like cold frames and cloches. These will extend the facilities for growing plants without creating difficulties. With some protection of this kind, the growing season can be extended. Seeds can be sown earlier, half-hardy plants can be given a good start, tomatoes and onions ripened, late crops protected and some plants over-wintered. Alpines need protection from the rain in winter – they don't mind the cold but hate being wet.

The simplest way to encourage early growth is to use an inverted jam-jar – this works well over widely spaced seeds like sunflowers, marrows and runner beans. Glass or plastic cloches will help to warm the soil if they are placed over the planting area about a week before sowing, and this gives better germination. Glass cloches are more expensive than plastic, and may get broken, but they retain the heat better. Plastic 'tunnel type' cloches are lighter and easy to make, but they may be difficult to anchor in a high wind. The advantage of this kind of protection is that it can be moved from crop to crop as the need arises. It gives protection from the birds, and can be used over boxes or pots of seedlings, for intermediate care or hardening off, and is very useful for raised beds.

Cold frames are available, and it is useful to have two – one in a sunny place and one which is out of the sun. They can be raised to whatever level is convenient for working. The glass cover can be counterbalanced so that it is not heavy to lift. A plunge-bed – a place for the temporary care of plants in pots – is very useful and an alternative is to have an outdoor bench with some sort of capillary material. This can be given a cover of plastic when necessary.

Indoors, growing facilities can be extended by using heated propagators for early seed sowing or taking tender cuttings, exploring the possibilities of growing under fluorescent lights, and using terrariums. The simplest method of ensuring humid and more even conditions for plants, cuttings and seeds is to enclose them in a clear plastic bag. The plastic bag or its alternatives – an inverted clear plastic beaker or a lemonade bottle with the top cut off – is a tremendous help to the home gardener and it is mentioned frequently in the recipe section.

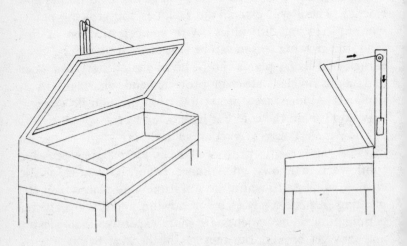

The lid of a cold frame can be counter-balanced for easy opening.

GARDEN TOOLS

Many people imagine that 'gardening for the disabled' implies buying a lot of special tools, but this is not true. All gardeners have their individual likes and dislikes and what suits one doesn't necessarily suit another. You need garden tools which do the job efficiently, are comfortable to handle and last a long time. It is worth paying a bit extra at the beginning to get good quality tools – but no one likes to make an expensive mistake. For any gardener, choosing something suitable from the bewildering range offered by different manufacturers may be difficult, but to the disabled gardener it may be a real problem.

Choosing garden tools which are comfortable in use is especially important if you have a disability. Spades and forks are made in different sizes, in stainless as well as ordinary steel and with a choice of handle. There are versions of tools such as rakes, hoes and secateurs which are lightweight, long or short-handled, or which offer some other possible advantage. There are ingenious weeders, planting aids, leaf-grabbers and all sorts of other equipment which could be helpful. But how do you find out which of them is going to suit you?

The local garden centre may not stock the full range, and almost certainly will not have the facilities for trying things out. Modern packaging creates additional difficulties – secateurs, for instance, are often sold in plastic bubble packs. How can you possibly try the grip and balance or assess the pressure needed to use them? Some people rely on the recommendations of friends, and are fortunate enough to be able to borrow equipment to try out in their own garden. Even so, there may be better tools on the market – or more suitable ones. To make a more informed choice and avoid buying 'a pig in a poke' here are some suggestions:

Find out what is available
Ask in garden shops or centres for illustrated catalogues or write to manufacturers asking for a catalogue and list of local stockists. New equipment often has a 'write-up' in gardening magazines.

A wheelbarrow that can be used one-handed. The Corrie Easywheeler has two wheels and is low, so that it does not tip over easily.

Decide what you need

It's no use buying a wheelbarrow for a balcony – the choice of equipment depends on the kind of gardening you intend to do. In your particular garden, what jobs need to be done, and which tools would help? Make a list of the things you need.

Consider your own needs

For some people it may be specially important to choose lightweight tools, or ones which can be used with only one hand. Gardeners with bad backs often prefer long-handled tools so that they can cope without bending. What are your special needs, and can you track down suitable versions of the tools you listed?

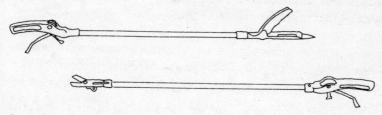

Gardening aids: the Baronet weeder and long-handled pruner.

Tools and equipment can be tried out at Horticultural Therapy's Demonstration Gardens. For details of your nearest Garden, telephone or write to Horticultural Therapy. You will find the address in the appendix.

Some garden centres, such as those at Syon Park and Barralets of Ealing, make a point of stocking the tools which are helpful to disabled gardeners and it is well worth asking your local garden centre about demonstration facilities.

Horticultural Therapy publish an eight-page booklet entitled 'Tools for Easier Gardening'. As well as providing valuable pointers on carrying out jobs in the garden, it also lists tools which have proved useful. The tools are classified according to the way in which they can be used – from a sitting position, with a weak grip, one-handed, or without bending the back. The list is based on work carried out by Mr A. S. White at Mary Marlborough Lodge, the Nuffield Orthopaedic Centre, Oxford.

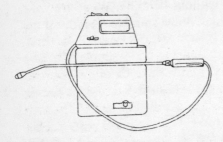

A power spray with a long tube – no need to lift watering cans.

The book *Gardening* in the series 'Equipment for the Disabled' is also based on this work. There are photographs and descriptions of a wide range of tools and garden equipment, including some which are home-made or have been adapted to suit people with a particular disability. Details of this and other publications can be found in the appendix.

Wolf tools for soil-tilling.

Adapting Tools

The simplest adaptation of garden tools is to pad the handles to give a better grip. A piece of foam plastic can be taped round, either at the end of a handle or halfway down the shaft of a rake or hoe. Plastic or rubber handlebar grips come in various sizes, from toy tricycle to motorcycle size, and these can be fitted over the ends of handles. Fixing an extra handle halfway down the shaft of a fork or spade makes it possible to dig from a wheelchair or reduces the need for bending.

Some garden tools and equipment can be used in different ways – using a bulb planter to dig the holes for peat blocks, for instance. To avoid lifting watering cans, an electrically powered or pressure sprayer with a long tube and nozzle could be used.

There is room for a lot of ingenuity in using simple domestic items. For instance, there are many ways in which you can scoop up sand or pebbles. If a trowel is heavy to hold, a plastic flour scoop may be lighter. Is the handle too small? Then try padding it out with plastic foam held in place with rubber bands – or use an empty tin which does not demand such a closed grip to hold it. Make sure, of course, that the tin has been opened cleanly, with no sharp edges. A plastic cup may be used in the same way. A big scoop can be made by cutting down a plastic one-gallon orange cordial container – the sort with a built-in handle.

Adapting tools sometimes requires a certain amount of ingenuity or engineering skill. Help of this kind is available from an organisation called REMAP which has panels of volunteers willing to design and make one-off aids to solve the specific problems encountered by some disabled people. For addresses of Regional Organisers write to:
REMAP (Rehabilitation Engineering Movement Advisory Panels), 25 Mortimer Street, London W1N 8AB. (071-637 5400).

PLANTING INDOORS – MOVING OUT

If it is too difficult to go out of doors, it is still possible to plant up pots which can be put outside by someone else. Just make sure that the pots or any version of the container-on-wheels have drainage holes or they will get water-logged when it rains.

Several plants can be grown in a large pot, or pots can be grouped. Standing them on a drainage tray holding pebbles or gravel ensures free drainage, and the plants benefit from the extra humidity of being grouped together.

A row of pots can be put on a 'windowsill tray' of gravel behind a row of bricks or stones. If the pots are assorted sizes, small pots can be raised by supporting them on half-bricks, or putting them in a larger pot filled with pebbles to the right height, or on an inverted plant pot.

Chimney pots or sections of drain-pipe can be used as supports for large pots. Hanging baskets need not be hung up – they can be supported on chimney pots or pipes like the one opposite, and then they are very easy to tend.

Vegetable-growing can also be managed if a growing-bag is put onto a flat trolley. Using one of the special growing-bag trays will prevent too much mess if you want to wheel it in and out. Planting indoors and putting the pots outside is also a great help in bad weather. When you are running a once-a-week programme there is a problem in getting plants transferred at the right time. You could be unlucky with the weather on your particular day with the group, and this could delay planting out, perhaps for two or three weeks. Young plants left over-long at this stage in seed trays or small pots get weak and spindly, and may never recover from the check to their growth. It would be better to put them into pots with more room to

grow, and with fresh potting compost to give them nourishment. The pots could be put on trays, or in tomato boxes, and popped outside to wait for better weather for final planting in the garden.

It is also possible to "garden from indoors" if pots can be set amongst permanent planting in the garden. For instance, in a rockery, it is possible to wedge pots between rocks, or surrounded by plants such as aubretia or saxifrage so that the pots do not show. A continuous display can be kept up, changing the pots when necessary, perhaps with bulbs in the spring, and geraniums in the summer. Planting of a bed can be cleverly arranged so that the basic maintenance is minimal, using ground-cover plants such as lambs-ear (stachys lanata) ivies, etc., with half-buried pots providing special interest. A raised bed which is temporarily out-of-use when a gardener is house-bound can be treated in this way – a scattering of fast growing annuals can form the background to a few special pots. A large out-door container can have a permanent planting of pretty ivies to trail over the edge or climb up a trellis. The ivies provide useful cuttings as well as making a natural background in which to set the pots. Small conifers and winter-flowering heathers also make a display in the cold months and form a good background for small pots of snowdrops and early spring flowers.

This 'pot method' makes it possible for a gardener to organise the outside work from indoors – merely asking someone else to exchange the pots. Even for more active gardeners, it is a great relief to cut down on the amount of work which it is necessary to do on cold, wet days.

POTTING COMPOSTS

A well-balanced potting compost is essential for growing indoor plants and for filling hanging baskets and some outdoor containers. Garden soil is not suitable, as it may contain worms and grubs, weed seeds and disease spores, as well as being of uncertain fertility. Potting composts are sterilised and the essential nutrients are included in the correct ratios for good plant growth.

There are two main kinds of compost:
1. Loam-based composts such as John Innes.
2. Peat-based composts such as Levington.

In addition there are very light, clean potting materials such as vermiculite granules, and different compost mixtures for plants with special needs such as cacti and tropical plants.

John Innes compost is prepared in three strengths, numbers 1, 2 and 3, depending on the amount of fertiliser that has been added to the basic mixture.

No. 1. is suitable for seed-sowing and small seedlings.

No. 2. is for established plants.

No. 3. is for plants which need to make rapid growth and for larger pot plants.

The loam used is usually a high-quality soil from mature meadowlands, which is sterilised before adding to peat and sand in the ratio 7:3:2. Unfortunately, due to the scarcity of good loam, there is considerable variation in the John Innes mixture from different suppliers. With any loam-based compost it is wise to try a small amount first before buying a large quantity.

Peat-based composts or 'soil-less' composts as they are often called, are produced by a number of well known firms. Some are sold as an all-purpose compost – others are sold in specific grades for seed sowing, taking cuttings or potting older plants. In choosing, read the instructions and ask for leaflets. The leaflets are often very well produced with illustrations of planting techniques and useful advice on cultivation. If you are in any doubt about which compost to use write to the manufacturer.

The composts are sold in plastic bags, already slightly moist. Keep this moisture by folding over the top of the bag after use. One or two bulldog clips or spring clothes pegs will hold it down.

Compost for cacti and succulents contains much more grit or sand, since good drainage is essential. Forest plants and ferns need a compost with a high humus content. Where a light clean material is of prime importance, potting substances such as Perlite or Vermiculite are invaluable.

Perlite is an extremely light, white, granular substance formed by heat-expansion of volcanic rock. It is sterile and can be used alone for germinating seeds or rooting cuttings, or with added nutrients for growing plants.

Holding moisture and yet draining freely, it is a useful addition to other composts. Perlite can also be used as a capillary material in plant-trays. Before using perlite, sprinkle it with water as it is very dusty when dry, and could be irritating. As a long-term growing medium, or as capillary material, it sometimes grows algae – this can be discouraged by watering with a weak solution of algaccide or one teaspoonful of Jeyes Fluid to one gallon of water.

Vermiculite is a form of mica which has been heated and exploded into small flakes. It is sterile and very light, and has the property of holding moisture whilst remaining open and porous. It is very good for seed-sowing and cuttings, but contains no plant food and rooted cuttings must soon be transplanted into normal compost.

If composts are altogether unsuitable, it is possible to explore hydroponic methods – growing plants in water which has added nutrients. Most good books on indoor gardening explain the techniques required.

COMPOST TRAYS

It is necessary to have something to hold a fairly large amount of compost when potting-up or seed-sowing. In a permanent potting area, trays can be made from wood, but you may need something which is fold-away – or even throw-away.

The Bricol Compost Tidy is made from plastic, lightweight but strong, and can be very quickly assembled. It can be used on a table top or work bench and then folded flat for storage.

A home-made version can be cut from a grocery box. Because the compost is moist and the box is only cardboard, it may have to be thrown away at the end of the afternoon. A shallow box can be used, simply by cutting off one of the long sides. Alternatively, two trays can be made from a deep box by cutting it in half vertically.

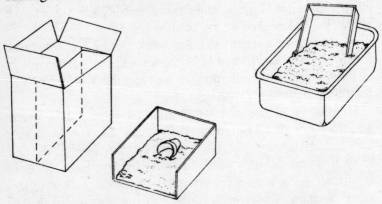

A plastic washing up bowl will hold compost – the rectangular ones are best, especially when filling seed trays. An old meat-roasting tin can be used, or anything else which is large enough to hold the amount of compost required and gives room to manoeuvre.

Of course, an ordinary tray can be used to stand pots on and catch the spills if necessary.

SEED SOWING

The problem most often mentioned by disabled people is the difficulty of sowing seeds. There are many ways of tackling this:

Avoidance

One way of by-passing the problem is to grow only those plants which can be reproduced by other means! Some indoor gardeners never grow anything from seed, relying entirely on propagation by cuttings. There are a great many outdoor plants – especially shrubs and perennials – which can be propagated in this way. Some plants can be increased by division into small clumps. This is one way of multiplying perennials like chives and primulas. Bulbs such as daffodils often multiply themselves and only occasionally need taking up and spacing out.

Another way of avoiding the problem is to buy young plants from a nursery or garden centre. Plants such as lettuce, runner beans and marrows are readily available and a great many hardy and half-hardy annuals can be bought either in individual containers or trays. Perennials and small shrubs are often container grown and can be transplanted easily. Wallflowers and cabbage plants can be bought for planting out in the autumn. So it is possible to have a garden without ever sowing a seed.

Choosing Big Seeds

Big seeds are the easiest to handle. They can be sown singly and present fewer problems in spacing and the later thinning of seedlings.

There are some plants which have very big seeds, like avocados and horse-chestnuts, and there are quite a few others which have seeds large enough to handle singly, such as beans, peas and marrows. Some flowers, such as sunflowers and nasturtiums, also have seeds which are large. Bulbs, although they are not seeds, provide the same excitement of planting something in the earth which develops into a plant. There are many different sizes of bulbs, and bulbs for all seasons. Two of the biggest – colchicum and amaryllis – are amongst the easiest to grow.

The colchicum (or 'autumn crocus') which is usually in the shops in August, does not even need soil. It will grow on a saucer and produces an astonishing number of flowers without leaves. The bulb can then be planted out in the garden, where it will produce big leaves in the spring.

Amaryllis (or hippeastrum) bulbs are often packaged with pots and compost ready to plant, and can be found in the shops from October to January. All that is needed is to plant the bulb in compost and keep it in a good light in a warm room, watering when necessary. Though they are expensive, the results are so spectacular that one or two amaryllis bulbs are well worth buying.

In the vegetable garden, onion sets are bulbs which one can think of as 'big seeds'.

Sowing Small Seeds

There are many disabilities which make the sowing of small seeds a difficult task. Some people are visually handicapped, some cannot manage the fine hand control which is required, and others lack the spatial awareness necessary for sowing seeds evenly. Handicapped gardeners are not alone; many people find the sowing of seeds a problem and manufacturers and seedsmen are constantly bringing helpful products onto the market.

Sowing seeds too thickly is wasteful; seedlings which grow too close together have to be spaced out, either by pulling out or cutting off the unwanted seedlings ('thinning'), or by replanting them at wider intervals ('pricking out'). These tasks

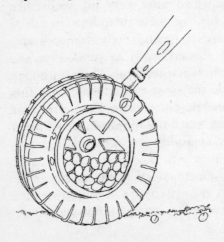

A long handle on the Wolf seed-sower is a help to the gardener who cannot bend.

require skill, dexterity and patience and may prove especially difficult for the handicapped gardener.

There are many methods of coping with the problem of sowing seeds with greater control. Seed sowing gadgets range from special wheels which space seeds individually at intervals, to simple 'pepper pot' shakers. Some people manage to tap the seeds from a folded piece of paper and others make use of such things as saccharine dispensers. Another way of controlling the flow of seeds is to mix them into a thickened liquid and squeeze them out in a line (see Fluid Sowing, April, page 91).

Directing seeds into evenly spaced holes may be helpful.

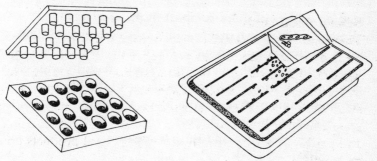

The Bricol seed-sowing device consists of a plastic shield with slots which fits over a seed tray. Similar seed tray tops can be made with spaced holes and blind gardeners can find these very useful. A home-made seed-positioner can be made from a lidded margarine pot (see April seed-sowing notes).

This method still involves pricking out the seedlings at some stage, which many people would prefer to avoid. However, containers which have separate planting spaces enable seedlings to be grown on for longer and then transplanted with their roots intact. These can be made of expanded polystyrene, plastic, or compressed peat. Manufacturers of these propagating trays are listed in the Appendix.

Sowing seeds individually or in twos or threes in small blocks of compost is economical on seed and also cuts out the problem of thinning or of pricking out the small seedlings later. This method not only eliminates a difficult stage in handling; it also prevents a check to growth at this vital point. Japanese market gardeners have been using a similar technique for years, and most commercial growers are abandoning the labour-intensive method of pricking-out in favour of peat or compost blocks.

It is a particularly useful technique for anyone who cannot manage the fine control which is needed to pick up seedlings by their seed-leaves and re-plant them, for those with poor eyesight, or even those with too little time or patience! The blocks are much easier to plant out eventually, simple to space and count, and to transfer with less disturbance to the roots. Another advantage of growing in peat-blocks is that the timing of transplanting is less crucial, especially if the compost blocks stand on a layer of more compost in the seed tray.

Research has shown that for some crops multiple-seeding of blocks gives very good results. There is no need to thin to a single seedling – all the plants will grow to maturity and give a normal yield. Carrots will not be successful, but the following maximum number of seeds to a block apply to:
- Leeks and Onions – 3 seeds
- Celery, Sweetcorn and Bush Tomatoes – 3 seeds
- Cabbage – 2 seeds
- Beetroot – 1 cluster

Similarly, seeds can be sown in Jiffy 7s, which are pelleted peat pots which make a solid block of peat when soaked in water, or in peat pots which have to be filled with seed compost. Like peat blocks, these can be planted directly into the soil in due course. Plastic pots or waxed paper cups can also be filled with compost and used for seed-sowing, but the cup must be removed on transplanting.

Sowing seeds, either out of doors or into trays or individual containers, is also more controlled if the seeds themselves are made easier to handle. *Pelleted seeds* are seeds which have been coated to make them larger. Do not sow as deeply as uncoated seeds and keep the soil very moist or the water will not penetrate and allow the seed to germinate. To prevent the soil from drying out, cover with polythene but remove it as soon as seedlings appear. *Seed sticks* are like wide cardboard matches, with three or four seeds to a stick, and they are simply

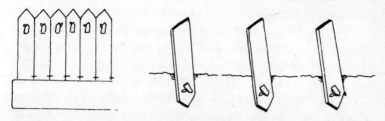

stuck into the desired growing place to the marked depth. *Seed strips* have ready-spaced seeds between layers of paper tape which dissolves after planting.

Picking up seeds a few at a time can be managed on the tip of a moistened toothpick or plastic plant label. Very fine, dust-like seed, such as that of petunias, is a problem to most gardeners, and one solution is to mix it with fine light-coloured sand. This 'dilutes' it and allows you to see where it has been sprinkled on the surface of the seed-compost.

These notes may have been sufficient to indicate some methods of overcoming the problems of seed-sowing, but individual gardeners often find other solutions. For instance, a funnel can be used to control the placing of seeds in peat blocks or in a seed tray. Those who cannot bend may find a long tube very useful for sowing large seeds out of doors, and there are many other ideas which develop spontaneously in response to particular problems. Improvisation and the exercise of ingenuity in overcoming problems may be valuable experiences in themselves and lead to a great sense of achievement.

Finally, from the point of view of an occupational therapist seed-sowing may present opportunities for exercising hand and eye co-ordination or fine muscle control, for assessment of ability or perseverance.

FERTILISERS

Compound fertilisers contain all three main plant foods – Nitrogen, Phosphate and Potash, known as N, P, K respectively – and sometimes include trace elements as well. Numbers are given on the label and they give the proportions of these principal ingredients, though it is not always certain that they will be in a form easily assimilated by the plants. The numbers also give an indication of the strength of the fertiliser. National Growmore, for instance, has equal quantities of N, P, K (7:7:7) and is a good general fertiliser for the garden. Apply at the rate of 50gm per square metre (1½ ozs per sq yard) for flowers, etc., and 100gm per square metre (3 ozs per sq yard) for vegetables. Certain fertilisers have different proportions – lawn fertiliser, for instance, is high in Nitrogen, which encourages leaf growth, and rose fertiliser is high in Potash, which is good for flowers and fruit. Phosphate encourages root development.

For the sake of simplicity, problems of storage or practical difficulties in application, it may be best to stick to one type of

FERTILISERS				
Fertiliser	Form	N Nitrogen	P Phosphorus	K Potassium
NATIONAL GROWMORE	GRANULES	7	7	7
PHOSTROGEN	POWDER	10	10	27
PHOS (TRO) TABS (PLANTOIDS)	TABLETS	8	11	23
BABY BIO	LIQUID	10.6	4.4	1.7
BIO PLANT FOOD	LIQUID	6	6	7
KERIGROW	LIQUID	6	4	4
SANGRAL	POWDER	15	15	30
FISONS LIQUINURE	LIQUID	8	4	4
FISONS TOMORITE	LIQUID	4	4.5	8
JOBES FLOWERPOT SPIKES	STICK	4	12	4
JOBES HOUSEPLANT SPIKES	STICK	10	4	5
JOBES TOMATO SPIKES	STICK	8	24	8
GEEST POKON	SACHETS CONTAINING POWDER	16	21	27
NUTRICELL	SLOW-RELEASE RESIN-COATED GRANULES	15	12	15

good general fertiliser, or perhaps one for the garden, and another kind for indoors. Choose something suitable for the plants you grow and which is convenient to apply.

Fertilisers come in various forms: granular or powder for dry application, powders which can be dissolved in water, and liquid fertiliser which has to be diluted. Disabled people may have difficulty in measuring out powdered or liquid fertiliser or in coping with accurate dilution or application. Fertiliser can also be found in tablet form or as sticks to be pushed into the soil. Foliar feeding – spraying the fertiliser onto the leaves – is also a possibility. This gives a wide choice of coping with the problem of fertiliser application.

Follow the instructions exactly and use the amount recommended by the manufacturer. Giving extra fertiliser does not increase the benefit, and may harm the plants. Never give liquid fertiliser to a plant that is bone dry. Thoroughly water the plant first, then give some fertiliser the next day.

Do not store cartons or bags in a damp place or leave the top open after use. Where there is any danger of misuse fertilisers should be stored in a locked cupboard.

DRAINAGE

The usual drainage material is either crocks (the broken-up remains of old clay plant pots) or stones, which may be anything from stones picked up in the garden to pebbles or gravel of various sizes. Do not put a flat stone or crock directly over a drainage hole, which will block it. Use a piece of crock, concave side down, or just odd shaped stones to let the water through.

Drainage material should be clean. It is no use scrubbing the pots and using sterile potting compost and then importing disease with the drainage material – wash it if necessary. Store pebbles and gravel in bags, not heaped on the ground where they will collect worms and woodlice.

If crocks or stones are not available, and you need to provide drainage or to prevent compost from dropping out of big holes at the bottom of a pot then crumple up an old nylon stocking or a small plastic net bag (used for nuts, oranges, etc.). In a larger container you can use one of the plastic net bags used for carrying vegetables such as onions, cabbages and sprouts. Greengrocers usually throw these bags away. This will ensure drainage, but if you want to water by means of capillary matting remember that the pots must be filled only with compost.

Some books advise separating the soil from the drainage layer with anything from old turf to a layer of leaves. This may defeat the object of using sterile compost and is not essential in containers which are replanted regularly. Containers which are used for more permanent planting do need something to stop the soil from working down and blocking the drainage. Hygiene in this case is not so important, but avoid using anything which would rot down over a period of time. Some nylon mesh or a few layers of old garden netting would work quite well.

Plastic pots and soilless potting compost are very light – sometimes it is wise to use some stones in the bottom, not only for drainage but for stability, so that a top-heavy plant does not fall over.

WATERING

In dry weather it is better to give the ground a thorough soaking once a week than to water every day. It is surprising how much water it takes to moisten more than the top inch or two of soil.

Do not water in the middle of the day whilst the sun is shining – drops on leaves and flowers will act as magnifying glasses and burn the plant. This applies to indoor plants as well as those in the garden.

For indoor plants, use water which has been standing in a bowl or jug for a while so that it is at room temperature. This also allows some of the chlorine to evaporate. Don't give your indoor plants a shock with water straight from the cold tap.

Soft water is safest – some of your plants may be lime-haters – or the minerals in the soil may build up with repeated watering and evaporation. Collect fresh rainwater – but don't risk bringing in pests or diseases with water from a rain barrel.

Other ways of obtaining soft water are to save the ice when defrosting the fridge, or use the left-over boiled water from the kettle – let both of these stand until the water is at room temperature, of course.

Cut down on watering in the winter – unless central heating causes plants to dry out very quickly.

Too much watering can

a. Waterlog the roots of the plant, causing leaves to yellow and drop off.
b. Make plants weak and 'leggy'.
c. Make a lot of growth and leaves, but few flowers.

Plants which are too dry wilt and the tips of the leaves turn brown.

Watering the Easy Way

It is not always necessary to water plants individually. There are ways of grouping them which save time and trouble, especially if water can be taken up into the pots from below by capillary action. You can make a tray filled with sand or Perlite or something similar, or use capillary matting.

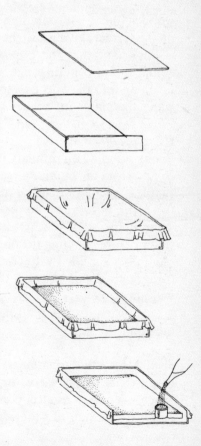

Making a sand tray

A wooden surface can be made into a tray by nailing on slats of wood as a rim and lining it with a single sheet of tough polythene. Fill it with sand, and sink a small clay pot or bit of drainpipe to touch the bottom of the tray. You can pour water through this without disturbing the sand. A plastic or metal tray could be used instead of a

A sand tray provides humidity as well as watering the plants.

wooden one. First soak the sand and then stand potted plants on the surface, giving a slight push to make them bed firmly. It is important that the pots are without crocks, so that the compost they contain is in contact with the sand. Water is then taken up into the pots by capillary action. There is no need to water the plants individually.

Using capillary matting

Plants standing on capillary matting can take up moisture and benefit from the humidity created around them. The method is simple – the matting can be cut with ordinary household scissors to fit the bottom of the drainage tray, trough, saucer, etc. Thoroughly soak the matting and then drain away surplus water before standing the plants on it. Again it is vital that the plant pots are filled with compost and do not have a drainage layer of crocks or gravel at the bottom, or the capillary action will not work.

Add water to the matting as required, so that it remains moist all the time.

Semi-Automatic Irrigation

In a greenhouse, conservatory or even on an outdoor growing bench, capillary matting can be used to create a semi-automatic system of watering.

The method is as follows:
1.   Ensure that the surface of the growing bench is solid and level, so that the capillary matting has the necessary support.
2.   Fix a length of 4 in plastic guttering with end caps to form a trough at the end of the bench (or along the front if that is more convenient).
3.   Cut a piece of polythene sheet to the size of the bench, leaving an extra bit all round (2.5 cm or 1 in is sufficient).
4.   Cut capillary matting to the size of the bench, allowing 10 cm (4 ins) extra at the trough side to allow the end of the matting to lie in the trough.
5.   Soak the matting completely, allowing surplus water to drain away. Lay it on the bench with the end in the trough. Fill the trough with water.
6.   Place the pots in position on the matting.
7.   The matting will take up water as required from the trough. Capillary action transmits the water evenly throughout the length of the bench. Add water to the trough as required, so that the matting remains moist at all times.
NOTE: An inverted bottle of water, clamped at the surface-level of the trough, will keep this system going for longer.

Automatic Watering
There are numerous ways – both home-made and commercial – in which water can be fed automatically to capillary matting. The water in the trough can be kept topped up by a water-

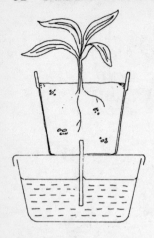

Automatic watering: a margarine pot with a lid can be used with a wick.

supply controlled by a valve. Some people use an old lavatory cistern with a ball-valve.

Misting

Misting is a very fine water-spraying of flowers or plants to counter a dry atmosphere or to keep cuttings moist whilst rooting. Do not mist spray when the sun is shining directly on to the plant. Use water at room temperature and mist in bursts, holding the nozzle of the sprayer about 45 cm (18 ins) from the plant. Flower arrangements and miniature gardens may need daily spraying. Never mist cacti or succulents, or any plant with hairy or downy leaves, such as an African Violet.

WEEDING

Weeding is a great problem for inexperienced gardeners. It is not easy to distinguish between the seedlings of plants and those of weeds. Recognising fully grown weeds may not be difficult but by the time they are mature it is too late! Gaining sufficient familiarity with leaf-shape and texture, particularly in the immature stages, is not easy for new gardeners. One way of avoiding this difficulty is to grow things in pots or peat blocks and then plant out in freshly hoed ground. This gives the plants a start – they can grow strong without competition and are then large enough to be easily distinguished from weed

Weeds and weed seedlings. *Left*: plantain; *right*: dandelion. Experience will teach you to recognize weeds before they grow too big.

seedlings. This is particularly useful when growing things like onions or ornamental grasses; even experienced gardeners have been known to pull them up by mistake!

SPRAYS – PESTICIDES AND WEED-KILLERS
Using poisonous sprays in the garden is a matter of personal choice. They should, of course, be avoided where there is any danger of misuse in any way. But there is also the consideration of the effect on wildlife. One should be aware of the danger of killing birds and hedgehogs which feed on plants and insects which have been sprayed with toxic substances. Many nature lovers would prefer to control weeds and pests in other ways and many manufacturers these days make a point of producing a range of safe sprays.

LIGHT

In choosing positions for plants, both indoors and outside, remember that nearly all *flowering* plants require a lot of light. Some will only flower really well in direct sunlight. *Variegated* plants (i.e. with white and green, or yellow and green leaves) need more light than the plain green varieties of the same plant, as they need to make up for their lack of chlorophyll.

In positions with too little light, plants will not thrive and in an attempt to reach more light they become leggy and spindly.

Part Two

Gardening Recipes

This is intended to be a week-by-week programme. The activities are divided into months – so every third month you will find an extra week's activities included, to take account of the fact that months are not an exact four weeks. Christmas week is assumed to be a holiday.

January

Week One
Sprouting Seeds and Bean Sprouts

Launching the group into activity from the start is a good beginning, and this session is designed to show something about the way in which seeds germinate and grow, and to give quick results.

Seeds need some water, air and warmth to start them into growth (that is, to germinate).

Sprouting Seeds
You need: Cress seeds
A saucer or foil dish
Paper towel
Scissors
Water

Method: 1. Fold the paper towel into four.
2. Cut to fit the dish.
3 .Pour on water to soak the towel.
4. Pour off the water.
5. Sprinkle with cress seeds – they need to be close together and evenly spread.

Afterwards

Water daily – make sure the paper towel keeps moist. When the seedlings unfold a pair of leaves the cress is ready to eat. Cut with scissors at the base of the stems and use in salad or sandwiches.

Suggestions

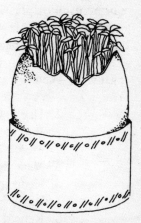

Cress can be grown in this way at any time of the year. Since it grows so quickly in a few days, light is not important – it can be grown anywhere in the room. Experiment – grow some on a windowsill, some in a dark place and compare the results.

Other seeds can also be grown in the same way – try alfalfa or sesame, or grains such as wheat and barley and various kinds of lentils.

For fun, grow cress on moist paper tissue packed into a clean eggshell. Draw a face on the shell with felt tip pen and support the shell on a cardboard 'collar' – cut a slice from the tube inside a kitchen roll – or simply stand it in an eggcup. The cress grows like 'hair' and can be cut with scissors.

Mung Beans

Bean sprouts grow quickly and you can use them to find out what effect different conditions have on the rate of growth of seeds. Try growing some in a jar on the windowsill, in a cold dark place, on a radiator shelf or on the top of the fridge, or in the airing cupboard.

The beans have a tough skin, so they need an initial soaking to start with, then only a little water to allow the seeds to breathe.

The beans are rinsed twice a day to keep them moist and prevent them from getting smelly. A net cover for the jar makes rinsing easier, or you can use a kitchen sieve. Use only a few beans and leave plenty of space in the jar for air. The cheapest way of buying mung beans is from a nature food store. For a group activity you could soak the beans overnight first (but take along some unsoaked ones to compare). Transparent jars may be used or plastic yoghurt pots with lids.

You need: Mung beans
            Jars with lids
            Water

Method: 1. Use a small quantity of beans.
            2. Put the beans in the jar with water to cover them. They need to soak overnight.
            3. Next day, drain off the water.
            4. Keep in a warm dark place (see notes above).
            5. Rinse in tepid water and drain.
            6. Repeat twice a day until the beans are about 5 cm (2 ins) long.

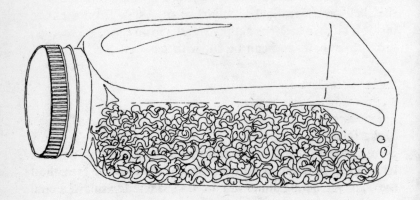

Recipes with Bean Sprouts
The bean sprouts do not need to be as long as the ones in the shops – they can be eaten when they are about 2 cm (¾ in) long, either raw or cooked. Wash the bean sprouts in a colander or sieve, letting as many of the seed cases wash off as you can.

Bean Sprout Salad
1 cup washed bean sprouts
2 cups finely sliced raw cabbage
1 medium-sized grated carrot
1–2 tablespoons French dressing or salad cream

Toss all the ingredients together in a large bowl.

Stir-fried Bean Sprouts
1 cup washed bean sprouts
1 tablespoon cooking oil
pinch of salt

In a thick saucepan or frying pan, heat the oil. When it starts to sizzle, add the bean sprouts and salt. Stir for about one minute over medium heat. Serve immediately.

Boiled Bean Sprouts
1 cup washed bean sprouts
1 cup water
pinch of salt

In a pan with a lid, bring the water and salt to the boil. Add bean sprouts and simmer for three minutes. Drain and serve.

Week Two
A Planning Session

This is a session for getting to know the members of the group, finding out about their gardening experiences and preferences, and planning ahead. How much ground is available and what can be done with it? (See notes on garden planning on page 26).

It is helpful to make a large plan of the garden and discuss how you can make the best use of the space available. Decide what needs to be done before spring comes. You may need to construct or buy things like plant troughs, window boxes or trellis for the walls and look out for suitable containers, so it's not too early to discuss ideas. Indoors you will need to make good use of the space on sunny windowsills and perhaps a table could be moved nearer to the window to give extra growing space.

More talk about planning can be stimulated by any of the following activities:

Sending for Seed Catalogues
You need: Paper, envelopes, stamps
              Ball point pens
              The gardening pages from Sunday newspapers

Find the advertisements from seed and plant firms. Tear them out, share amongst the group and write off for catalogues. (See also page 197 for addresses).

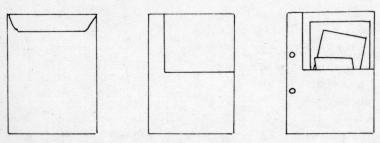

Using a manilla envelope to store leaflets.

Starting a Garden Scrap-Book
This can be a personal scrap-book or a group effort. Loose-leaved, it can be made from sheets of plain white or coloured paper, clipped into a large file cover and added to throughout the year. Paste in pictures cut from magazines or old seed catalogues, with notes about growing methods, hints and ideas. Make a pocket out of a large manilla envelope to hold leaflets. The scrap-book can be in the form of a diary recording the progress of the garden and individual achievements and include dates of sowing, transplanting and harvesting. Photographs taken throughout the year make good reminders of methods and stimulate discussion.

Making a Poster
You need:　A large sheet of paper
　　　　　　Felt pens
　　　　　　Old catalogues and magazines
　　　　　　Scissors
　　　　　　Paste

Design a poster around the name of the Club and give the date and time of meetings. Add drawings or paste on pictures cut from the magazines or catalogues.

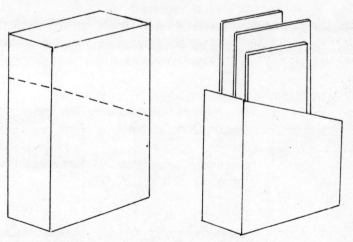

Cutting a cereal packet to make a box for catalogues.

A Garden Plan
You need: A large sheet of paper
             Pencil
             Ruler
             Felt pens

Draw a large plan to scale, discuss your ideas for planting and mark in on the plan. This can be made more pictorial with colourful drawings or pictures of flowers, vegetables and containers cut from magazines.

Gardening Books
Take along some well illustrated gardening books from the library and discuss favourite flowers and plants and methods of growing them. Plan a small library of your own.

Gardening Magazines
Buy some gardening magazines and see which ones you like best. Perhaps you will decide to subscribe regularly. Among those available are:

On sale in newsagents: Amateur Gardening
                        Garden Answers
                        Garden News
                        Greenhouse
                        Popular Gardening
                        Practical Gardening

By subscription: Gardening from 'Which'.
                  Monthly, but no issues in December and August. Bumper issues in April and October.
                  Consumers Association, 14 Buckingham Street, London WC2N 6DS.

                  Growth Point
                  Quarterly from the Society for Horticultural Therapy.

The Gardener
Braille or C.90 cassette, quarterly.
Available only to people registered as
blind.
Details from Miss Kathleen Fleet, 48 Tol-
carne Road, Pinner, Middlesex, HA5 2DQ.
(Telephone: 01-868 4026)

Visit a Garden Centre
An outing to a local Garden Centre can provide a great
inspiration. Look at plants, seeds, tools and collect leaflets –
some of these can be very colourful and informative.

All kinds of household containers can be saved to make useful pots for
planting.

Week Three
Pips and Stones

The joys of producing 'something for nothing' and watching things grow can become an absorbing hobby. There is an element of chance – not all pips or stones you find in fruit will prove to be fertile – but that provides excitement and a sense of achievement. The success rate will be increased by providing reasonable conditions for germination, and planting more than you need will give a margin for failure.

Citrus pips and the stones from fruits such as avocados, dates and lychees need greater warmth and moisture than seeds from temperate zones, so they need somewhere warm to germinate. A good place is the airing cupboard, or a shelf over a radiator. Enclosing the seeds in a moist atmosphere can be managed by germinating them in a screw-top jar or plastic pot with a lid, or putting the planting pot into a plastic bag. Even simpler, place the pips or stones in a plastic bag with some moist seed compost, or a peat/sand mixture, and seal it up.

Apple and pear pips will germinate at ordinary room temperature. Ripe pips are dark brown or almost black. Apples and pears which have been kept for a while are most likely to produce seeds which are ready to grow, so January is a good time to start them off.

Grape pips can also be germinated in the living room, and can be grown out of doors later.

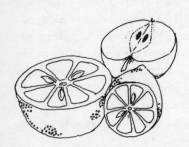

Cherry, plum and peach stones will germinate if they are over-wintered outside like acorns and horse-chestnuts (see September, Week Three).

None of the resulting plants can be guaranteed to produce fruits, or fruits exactly like their parent, but small trees make interesting pot plants, or material for bonsai growing. All kinds of citrus pips can be grown and some of the little trees may eventually bear scented blossom and fruit. Seville oranges are hardiest and germinate well, and the mandarins (including tangerines, clementines and satsumas) are the quickest to mature and will fruit in 30 cm (12 in) pots. Lemon pips will germinate at ordinary living room temperature.

You need: Pips and stones
Peat and sand (1 cup of each)
Pots/jars (with lids or plastic covers), or pots with plastic bags (self sealing or with twist-ties)
Water

Method:
1. Mix sand, peat and a small amount of water.
2. Squeeze the compost. If it will just hold together it is moist enough. If not, add more water.
3. Put a layer in the pots or jars.
4. Add pips or stones.
5. Cover with a layer of moist compost about 1 cm (½ in) deep.
   For grape pips, just cover with a thin layer.
6. Put on the lid, or enclose in plastic bag.
7. Put in a warm place. (see notes).

Aftercare

The roots will develop first, and then leaf-growth will start. Examine frequently – it is important to bring the seedlings into good light *as soon as any shoots emerge*. If only one or two have grown, dig them out (with a finger, table fork or any convenient tool) and pot them up individually, returning the rest of the pips to the warm spot to see if more will grow. Grow the plants in good compost in a warm light place, covered with a plastic bag at first, to retain moisture.

Week Four
A Pebble Pot

This is an attractive way of presenting cuttings of indoor plants which root easily in water. If a glass or transparent container is used it will allow the roots to be seen developing in the spaces between the pebbles. (Glass marbles can be used in place of pebbles.) The cuttings, when rooted, can either be grown on in the pebble pot or transferred into a normal growing medium – soil or potting compost.

A pebble pot can be started at any time of the year – and it is very useful to have one on the windowsill to receive the odd cutting. It is not easily knocked over so is useful to those with shaky hands or poor sight.

You need: A dish or jar deep enough to take at least a
5 cm (2 ins) layer of pebbles
Piece of charcoal
Pebbles or small stones
Cuttings of easily rooted plants
Water

Suitable plants are: Tradescantia (wandering jew)
Philodendron (sweetheart plant)
Chlorophytum (spider plant)
Plectranthus (Swedish ivy)
Rhoicissus (grape ivy)
Coleus

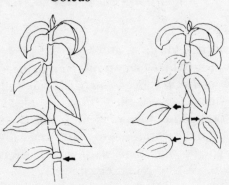

1. Take cuttings 7.5–10 cm (3–4 ins) long, below a leaf joint, stripping off the leaves on the bottom 5 cm (2 ins) of stem.
2. Put a piece of charcoal and a layer of pebbles into the container.
3. Wedge the cuttings into position, adding the rest of the pebbles to anchor them.
4. Add water to just below the top surface of the pebbles.

Aftercare
Keep in a light place, but not in bright sun.
Top up the level of water when necessary.
When the cuttings have rooted, feed regularly with liquid fertiliser once a month and the plants will go on growing.

Grow a Few Extra Cuttings

Since roots really develop best in darkness, good water containers for growing cuttings are Marmite or Bovril jars which are made of brown glass and are very stable. Brown pill bottles, either plastic or glass, can be used for individual cuttings. Coffee mugs, small jugs – almost anything you can fit on the windowsill will do. If you have problems preventing the cuttings from falling in, put a piece of kitchen foil over the top of the pot and pierce holes to push the cuttings through. These will be potted up in compost in February, Week Four.

February

Making a Root-Top Garden and Sprouting Potatoes

Root Top Garden
The tops of root vegetables, such as carrots, parsnips and turnips are usually thrown away but they will grow new leaves quite quickly. It is interesting to watch the development of the leaves and observe the differences in shape. With some stones to hide the vegetable bases these can look like a 'fern garden'.

If you are using kitchen throw-aways for a group activity make sure they are fresh and have at least one sample of each root vegetable for demonstration and recognition. Beetroot can also be used but this is not often obtainable from the kitchen as beet has to be cooked whole or it 'bleeds'. Buy small raw beetroot, slice off the tops and use the rest peeled and finely grated in salad.

Root vegetables bought in shops probably already have their leaves removed but garden vegetables may need trimming. Cut off the leaves, leaving about 6 mm (¼ in) of stem.

You need: Thick slices 1.2cm (½ in) from the tops of carrots, parsnips, small turnips, beetroot
A saucer or
shallow dish
Water
Clean pebbles
or stones (optional)

Method: Arrange the tops on the dish, add pebbles.
            Pour in water to halfway up the slices.

Aftercare
Top up water when necessary.

Sprouting Potatoes
As an interesting experiment a few potatoes can be grown in an
outdoor container or even in a plastic bag. (See March, Week
Three, Page 84). Potatoes grow best if they are 'sprouted' first;
that is, the shoots are allowed to develop before planting the
potato in the soil. Now is the time to start them off. If you are
buying seed potatoes, Maris Bard is a good early cropping
variety. Otherwise you can use potatoes from the greengrocer.

You need: 2 or 3 small potatoes
             Egg box

Method: Choose potatoes about the size of a large hen's egg
            and look for the 'eyes' – the indented buds which
            will develop into shoots.
            With the 'eyes' upwards, stand the potatoes in an
            egg box in a light place somewhere cool but frost
            free, e.g. on the windowsill of an unheated room.

Aftercare
Look at them occasionally and allow three shoots to develop
on each potato, rubbing off any extra ones. They will be
planted out about mid-March.

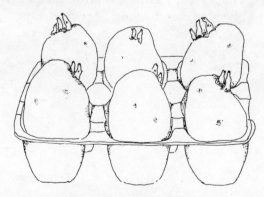

Week Two
Making the Most of Indoor Plants

Plants often look more effective and flourish better when grouped together. Choosing leaf shape and colours carefully, a most decorative effect can be obtained without the need for flowers. However, flowering plants can be included, and in order to keep up a continuous display they should be replaced when the flowers fade. The easiest way of doing this is to make the foliage arrangement in the large container and include the flowering plant *still in its pot*. Replacements in pots of the same size fit into the space, and plants can be bought, grown specially, or potted up and brought in from the garden for temporary display throughout the year.

One suggestion for a succession of blooms:
Snowdrops (from the garden); crocus (grown outdoors in pots); early tulips (indoors); primula; african violet; begonia; colchicum (autumn crocus); cyclamen; Christmas cactus.

Another idea is to 'plant' a narrow jar, test-tube or metal

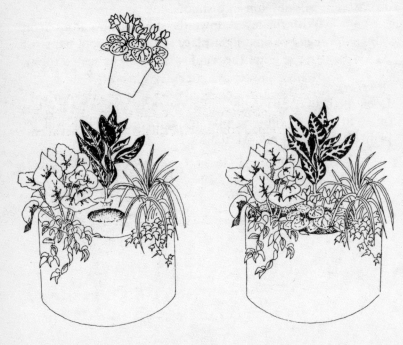

cigar container in the arrangement to hold fresh flowers. The flowers last well in the humidity of the surrounding foliage, and only a few flowers are needed to enliven a display. A few freesias, a branch of forced forsythia (see February Week Four, page 78) or a single horse-chestnut flower focus attention and appreciation in an arrangement like this. It is an encouragement to observe plant forms and perhaps will motivate outings into the garden or further afield to choose and collect fresh material.

Incidentally, this is a good way of keeping up interest in a display that, once planted, is otherwise rather static.

Choose plants which are compatible – that is, have similar requirements of light, heat and moisture. It would be no use planting a cactus with a fern as their needs are so different and one of them would be sure to die. There are, of course, less extreme cases, but it is useful to know something about the differing needs of plants. Grouping them sensibly will give you a longer lasting arrangement. This is a useful 'starting off' session which gives an opportunity to discuss the requirements and care of indoor plants.

A Foliage Arrangement
You need:　A large bowl or trough
　　　　　　Drainage material (crocks or gravel)
　　　　　　Potted plants, chosen from the chart overleaf (three or more according to the size of the bowl)
　　　　　　Pre-moistened compost (to fill in the space between the plants)
　　　　　　A mist bottle and water

Method: 1. Place 2.5 cm (1 in) of drainage material in the bowl.
2. Experiment with grouping the pot plants in the bowl to make an attractive arrangement.
3. Take the plants out of their pots and place in position.
4. Fill the spaces between with the extra compost, firming but not pressing too hard.
5. Spray mist over the plants.
6. Do not put into direct sun for a day or two.

Chart of Compatible Plants

These plants will grow in a cool room without much light:

Aspidistra
Cissus antarctica (kangaroo vine)
Fatshedera lizei (not variegated)
Fatsia japonica
Ficus pumila
Hedera (green ivy)
Rhoicissus rhomboidea (grape ivy)

These plants will grow in a warm room without much light:

Begonia rex (iron cross)
Cyperus (umbrella plant)
Ficus elastica decora (rubber plant)
Monstera deliciosa (cheese plant)
Neanthe bella (parlour palm)
Philodendron (sweetheart plant)
Sansevieria (mother-in-law's tongue)

These plants will grow in a cool room in good light:

Begonia semperflorens (fibrous-rooting begonia)
Campanula isophylla (bellflower)
Chlorophytum (spider plant)
Euonymous
Fatshedera lizei (variegated)
Hedera helix and Hedera canariensis (variegated ivies)
Hypoestes (polka dot plant)

Plectranthus australis (Swedish ivy)
Primula obconica
Setcreasea
Solanum capsicastrum (winter cherry)
Tradescantia (wandering jew)
Zebrina

These plants will grow in a warm room in good light:
Begonia rex
Beloperone guttata (shrimp plant)
Coleus blumei
Hippeastrum (amaryllis)
Impatiens sultanii (busy lizzie)
Iresine (blood leaf)
Peperomia magnoliaefolia (green and variegated pepper elder)
Saintpaulia (African violet)
Succulents

These are only a few of the common houseplants but it is very easy to find further information and there are many good books on houseplants.

Week Three

New Plants from Old – Taking Stem Cuttings

It is well worth learning the techniques of taking cuttings. It can become an addictive hobby – enthusiasts never go anywhere without a pair of secateurs and a plastic bag with a damp tissue inside.

Taking stem cuttings is described here but methods for semi-ripe, hardwood and root cuttings can be found in many gardening books.

Instead of preparing potting compost and filling pots, one could use prepared Jiffy 7s or peat blocks (see April Week Two, page 98).

Making a Cutting Compost

You need: 2 plastic pots with drainage holes
Peat – enough for one pot
Coarse sand – enough for one pot

Method: 1. Fill one pot with moist peat.
2. Fill one pot with sand.
3. Tip contents of both pots onto table and mix thoroughly.
4. Squeeze a handful – it should be just damp enough to hold together. If not, sprinkle with more water.
5. Fill the two pots with the mixture.
6. Level off, and then press the mixture down a little. This will leave about 1.2 cm (½ in) space at the top.

Taking Stem Cuttings:

You need: A healthy plant
Secateurs or a sharp knife
Prepared pots of compost
Rooting powder (optional)
Dibber
Water
Saucers or a draining tray
Clear plastic bag
Twist tie or rubber band

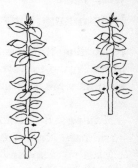

Method:

1. Choose healthy non-flowering stem tips of the parent plant.
2. Cut off 7–10 cm (3–4 ins) just below a leaf joint.
3. Take off the bottom leaves and any others on the bottom half of the stem.
4. Make a hole in the compost with a dibber.
5. Dip the end of the cutting into rooting powder and shake off any surplus (optional).
6. Insert the cutting to ⅓ of its depth and firm the compost round it.
7. Water and drain.
8. Stand on a drainage tray or saucer.
9. Cover with a plastic bag, either putting in the whole pot and closing with a twist tie, or inverting the bag over the pot and holding it with a rubber band round the pot.

NOTE: Blow air into the plastic bag, or keep it away from the cutting by supporting it on sticks pushed into the compost.

Aftercare

Water and liquid feed when necessary. Nip out the tips of shoots when they grow to 10–15 cm (4–6 ins) to make bushy plants.

Suitable Plants

Tradescantia, Philodendron, Iresine, Impatiens, Plectranthus, Ficus pumila.

Week Four
Blossoming Early and Potting Up

Blossoming Early
Most spring-flowering shrubs will flower early if brought indoors while still in bud.

You need: Branches showing plenty of flower buds (these are
the fat ones – smaller buds usually develop into
leaves).
Choose from the following:
Forsythia
Magnolia soulangiana or Magnolia stellata
Chaenomeles (Japonica or flowering quince)
Flowering Crab Apple
Flowering Cherry
Salix caprea (pussy willow)
Hazel Catkins (lamb's tails)
A bucket or a deep container
Tepid water
Large transparent plastic bag

Method: 1. Cut the branches on a day without frost.

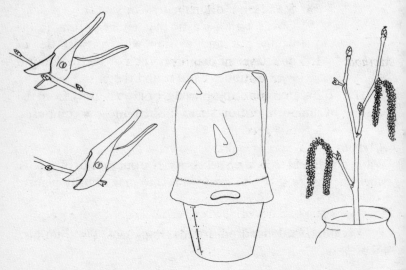

2. Crush the ends of the branches to help them to absorb water.
3. Stand in deep tepid water, and when it cools, cover the branches with a large inverted plastic bag.
4. Keep in a light cool place, out of direct sun until the buds show some colour.
5. Remove the plastic bag, and arrange the branches in a vase or with other flowers or plants in an arrangement.

NOTE: Early in March, bring indoors twigs of horse-chestnut with large sticky buds – just stand them in water. When the buds open the leaves gradually unfurl.

Potting Up

The spare cuttings which were rooted in water (January Week Four) are now ready for potting up.

You need: Pots with drainage holes
Potting compost or seed
compost (see last week)
Trowel or spoon
Water
Saucers or drainage tray

Method: 1. Put a layer of compost in the pot.
2. Hold the cutting in the pot and fill around it with compost.
3. Firm gently.
4. Water and drain.
5. Place in a warm room in a good light.

Aftercare
Plants in potting compost do not need fertilising for the first 4–6 weeks, but those in seed compost need a liquid feed after the first week.

March

Week One
African Violets (Saintpaulia ionantha) –
Care and Leaf Cuttings

African Violets are popular small indoor plants which flower almost all year round, and can be obtained in many shades of pink, blue and violet, with a great variety of petal shapes. There are frilled, double and crested flowers as well as the single form, and different types of leaf too. Building up a collection can become a fascinating hobby, and as African Violets root easily from leaf cuttings, it isn't expensive. There is plenty of scope for leaf-swapping with fellow enthusiasts. This is a plant which grows well under fluorescent lights, so it would give an introduction to 'light-gardening' techniques.

African Violets like plenty of light, but not hot sunshine; a humid atmosphere, but not standing in water; careful watering with tepid water and no cold draughts. When watering, it is best not to wet the leaves or to soak the crown of the plant, so either water with the spout of the can *under* the leaves, or stand the plant in water half-way up the pot for about an hour and then drain before putting back on the saucer. They grow well if the pots stand on small saucers on a tray of damp peat or wet pebbles to provide the necessary humidity. The compost needs to be moist but not soggy.

Taking Leaf Cuttings

You need: An African Violet plant
Pot with drainage holes
Rooting compost (or mix half peat, half sand)
Rooting powder
Dibber

Method:
1. Fill a pot with rooting compost to 1.2 cm (½ in) of rim.
2. From the plant, choose leaves that are firm, unblemished and look healthy. Leaves that are mature but not on the outer ring of leaves are the most successful.
3. Cut the leaf off neatly where it joins the plant.
4. Cut the leaf stem shorter if necessary, to 2–3 cm (¾–1 in) long.
5. Dip the end into rooting powder and shake off the excess.
6. Make a hole in the rooting compost with a dibber.
7. Put in the stem and press down the rooting compost, supporting the leaf clear of the surface. Repeat with more leaves. Planting round the edge of the pot about 1 cm (½ in) in will give the leaves support on the rim.

Aftercare
Keep the compost moist.

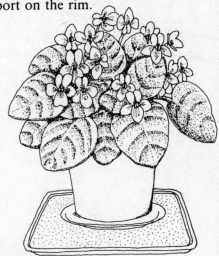

Week Two
Potting on Indoor Plants

When a plant is growing too big for its pot and the roots are becoming cramped, it needs to be transferred to a larger pot. Choose a pot which is only slightly larger than the previous one; too large a difference will result in a check to growth. This method of 'potting on' ensures that the plant is centred on the new pot and is at the right depth, and also that the fresh compost is not rammed down hard.

You need: Plants in 8 cm pots (3½ ins), ready to be 'potted on'
Clean 12 cm (5 in) pots – one for each plant
A spare empty 8 cm pot
Potting compost

Method: 1.   Put a little compost into the bottom of the 12 cm pot.

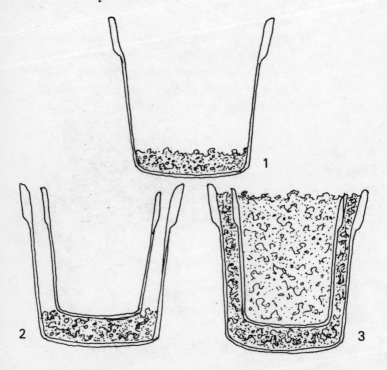

2. Place empty 8 cm pot inside the 12 cm pot, ensuring:
   - the rims of the two pots are level,
   - the 8 cm pot is central.
3. Fill the two pots with compost – smooth across the top with the side of the hand to remove surplus compost.
4. Remove the 8 cm pot. This leaves a neat planting hole, the correct size for the plant which has been grown in an 8 cm pot.
5. Now take the plant, remove the pot, and place the plant in the hole.
6. Tap the pot on the bench two or three times to settle the compost. If using a peat-based compost, do not firm.

4   5

Week Three
Potato Planting – Container Growing

The potatoes which were set to sprout last month (February Week One) should now be ready for planting. You need a large container at least 30 cm (1 ft) deep which has drainage holes. Anything will do – an old dustbin or bucket, wooden box or barrel or even a tough plastic bag with holes punched at the bottom. Obviously, the larger the container the more potatoes you can plant in it – reckon on giving each potato about 30 cm by 30 cm (a square foot) of surface, (e.g. one potato in a bucket, three in a dustbin).

The containers can be set out on a paved area or a balcony, preferably in a sunny spot, and raised up so that the drainage is free. It can stand on some old bricks or anything handy. If the container is rested on the soil, raising it is unnecessary.

A few crocks or stones at the bottom of the container will help drainage and keep the holes from clogging. Peat mixed with a granular fertiliser is suggested, but if that is difficult a liquid fertiliser may be used instead.

You need: A large container
              Drainage material (crocks or stones)
              Peat or peat mixed with soil
              Fertiliser – National Growmore (two level table-spoonfuls per potato)
              Water
              Sprouted potatoes

Method:
1. Check that the container has drainage holes.
2. Put in a layer of crocks or stones.
3. Moisten the peat (or mix moist peat and soil).
4. Mix in the fertiliser.
5. Put a layer of this mixture over the stones, filling one third of the container.
6. Plant the potatoes, shoots upwards, being careful not to knock the shoots off.
7. Cover with 10 cm (4 ins) of the peat mix.

8. Keep the rest of the peat mixture in a plastic bag for use later.

Aftercare
1. When green leaves appear add more peat to cover them – this protects the young leaves from frost.
2. Water when necessary.
3. Repeat the 'earthing up' whenever more leaves appear until the danger of frost is past. Then earth up to the base of the leaves until the container is almost full. The stems of the potato plant will grow longer and there will be more peat for the newly formed potatoes to grow in. This prevents them poking out and turning green.
4. As soon as the plant flowers (in July) you can start harvesting. Dig into the soil with a trowel and find out if the potatoes are big enough. You can harvest a few and leave the rest to grow a bit bigger.

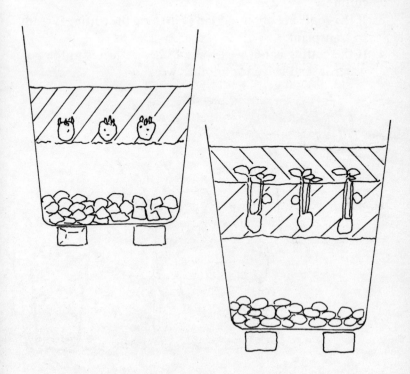

Week Four
Potting Rooted Cuttings

You need: Pots with drainage holes – as many pots as cuttings
Potting compost (pre-moistened and enough for
the number of pots)
Cuttings taken last month (see February Week
Three)
Water
Table fork or teaspoon

Are the Cuttings Rooted?

1. Look at the cuttings. Do they show any new growth? Tug
   gently at one of the cuttings – does it resist? Then the
   cuttings have rooted.
2. Dig carefully into the pot with fork or spoon and remove the
   cutting.
3. If the roots are about 2.5 cm (1 in) long the cutting is ready
   to transplant.
4. If the cutting is not well rooted, then return it to the pot,
   water it, and leave for another week.

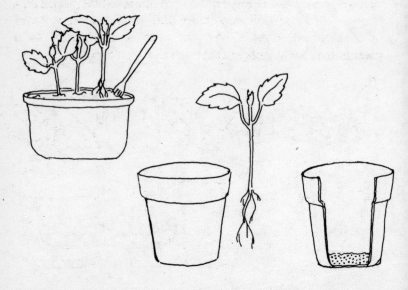

Potting
1. Hold the cutting against the pot and estimate how deep to fill the pot below the roots.
2. Put that amount of compost in the pot.
3. Hold the plant on top of the compost, making sure it is centred in the pot.
4. Add more compost all round the plant to fill the pot.
5. Tap the pot on the table. The compost should settle to about 1 cm (½ in) below the rim of the pot. Add a little more if necessary.
6. Place pot on saucer or drainage tray.
7. Water. Leave to drain, then tip out surplus water from saucer or tray.

Aftercare
Water the plants normally, but give no fertiliser for the first four weeks. Good potting compost contains enough fertiliser to maintain the plants at first.

Shading Newly-Potted Plants
Seedlings cuttings and any plants that have recently been disturbed in any way (transplanted, re-potted or planted into containers) should be shaded from strong sunshine. Stand on a non-sunny windowsill, in a shady part of the garden, or cover in the hottest part of the day with a newspaper. In a greenhouse, adjustable shades such as roller-blinds are useful.

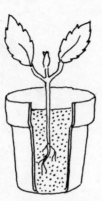

Week Five
Strawberries for Autumn Fruiting

This is a good introduction to techniques for preparing outdoor beds or containers for plants or seed-sowing, so the ground intended for April-sowing of annuals and vegetables can be prepared at the same time.

You need: A sunny space in garden bed or border, raised bed or container

Fertiliser (see notes on page 45)

Garden fork, rake, trowel

Strawberry plants – the perpetual kind (good varieties are Gento and Hampshire Maid) – preferably in peat pots with the tips of the roots just showing through the pots. Plants can be obtained from a local garden centre, or from Ken Muir or Chris Bowers. (See Appendix, page 198)

Preparing the Soil in the Garden
1. Sprinkle the area with the recommended amount of fertiliser (100 gms per sq metre or 3 ozs per sq yard).
2. Dig the soil, break up lumps with a fork and rake it level.
3. Firm the soil by treading over it – shuffling the feet to firm

the whole area to be planted in the garden bed. Firm soil in containers with the back of a trowel.

4. Water if dry, and leave to soak in.

Planting

1. The strawberry plants should be about 20 cm (8 ins) from the edge of the bed and 45 cm (18 ins) between plants (see page 25 for measuring sticks).

2. Use a trowel or bulb planter to make the planting holes. Check the depth of planting – the soil should be just over the top of the peat pot when the plant sits in the hole. If the plants are not in peat pots, gently spread out the roots, and hold the plant at the right level when filling in the hole.

3. Replace soil round the plant, firming with the trowel.

4. Water the plants well (about a litre, or nearly 2 pints of water for each plant) with a watering can.

For those unable to lift a full-sized watering can or for over-enthusiastic waterers, it is a good idea to have a large container of water and a jug. Pour enough water for each plant into a small-size watering can and water the plants one at a time.

Aftercare

If no rain falls the plants may need watering again next week. No further watering is necessary, except in dry spells. When the first flower buds appear, nip them off – the plant needs to grow strong before forming fruit. The second flowering can be left to form fruit. Next year, the plants can flower and fruit normally.

April

Seed Sowing Techniques

Although some seeds can be sown earlier, April is the main month for this activity. It may be too cold to start sooner, and in any case, the programme will be dependent on the weather. Look at the seed packets and decide on your priorities.

Apart from vegetables and flowers for the garden, you will need to sow things like herbs and everlasting flowers to use for craft work later.

The following basic techniques can be used in the weekly sowing sessions for this month.

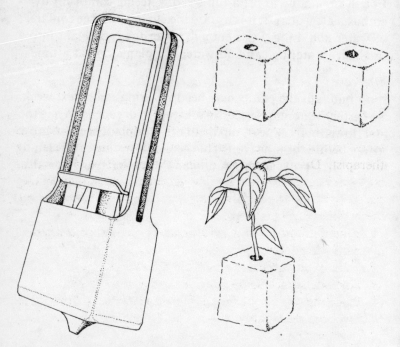

Peat blocks make an excellent medium for seed sowing.

Sowing Seeds in Blocks

You need: A blocking tool (Fisons Blockaid)
              Levington Blocking Compost
              A bowl or bucket
              Tepid water
              Seed tray
              Peat

Method:

1. Mix the blocking compost with tepid water to a moist, sticky consistency (but not too wet).
2. Fill the Blockaid with moist compost and press the blocks out on to a clean surface. Arrange the blocks close to each other in a clean seed tray, on a layer of moist peat.
3. Seeds can be sown in the hollow in the centre and covered with peat. The blocks can also be used for seedlings and cuttings.
4. Whilst the seeds or plants are growing, keep well watered.
5. When the roots begin to show through the sides of the peat block it is time to pot on or to plant out.

Fluid Sowing of Pre-Germinated Seeds

The simple technique of 'Fluid sowing of pre-germinated seeds' could become a useful and important tool for the therapist. Disabled people often have problems in handling and spacing small seeds. By first germinating and then mixing the seeds in wallpaper paste, and squeezing them out like icing, the problems can be overcome.

1. Line the bottom of a sandwich box, or similar container, with strong absorbent paper.
2. Soak with water and drain off the excess.
3. Sprinkle seeds evenly over the surface.
4. Place the top on the box, or cover with plastic film. Keep the box reasonably warm, (NOT as hot as an airing cupboard).
5. Check the seeds every day to see how many have

germinated. Allow the roots of smaller seeds, such as lettuce to roughly reach 6 mm (¼ in), those of larger seeds can be allowed to reach up to 1.2 cm (½ in). This will take from one to five days.

6. Remove the seeds by washing them into a fine strainer.
7. Make up some carrier jelly; this can be a proprietary product, or Polycell Regular Wallpaper paste at half normal strength, (avoid any paste containing fungicides).
8. Sprinkle the seeds onto half the paste, add the other half, then mix gently but thoroughly to give an even distribution.
9. Use cake icing equipment or a strong polythene bag with the corner cut off – (not too much!) Experiment to see how thickly the seeds are emerging – use a wider nozzle or cut more off the polythene bag if the seeds are too widely spaced.
10. Extrude into a shadow drill.
11. Cover with soil. Water if it is dry.

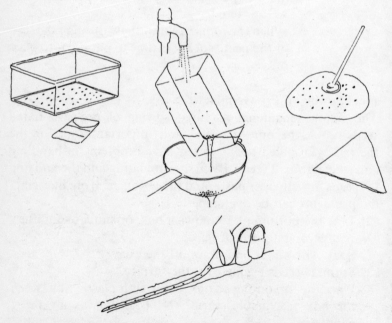

Fluid sowing. Germinating the seeds in a plastic box, rinsing them, mixing them into a gel and using a plastic bag for sowing.

Don't store seeds in the jelly for more than a few hours, and as with normal sowing don't allow the seeds to dry out.

This technique not only has the advantage of ease of handling and spacing, but also allows you to see the germinated seeds, and it gives a faster, more even, and reliable germination. This method could be used without pre-germination for sowing seeds indoors or out.

Growing Seeds in Peat Pellets

You need: Peat pellets (Jiffy 7s)
Water in a bucket or bowl
Shallow container or seed tray
Peat
Newspaper or paper towel
Seeds

Method: 1. Soak the pellets in water until they expand (about 15 minutes).
2. Handle as little as possible whilst in water.
3. At the bottom of the shallow container or seed tray place a layer of peat or several layers of newspaper or paper towel.
4. Moisten well.
5. Arrange the peat pellets on top, close to each other but not touching.

6. Small seeds should be placed on the top or large seeds can be pushed deeper into the pellet – see seed packet instructions about sowing.
7. Cover the seed with a little moist peat.
8. Enclose the whole container with a plastic bag or invert an empty seed tray on top.

Aftercare
As soon as the seeds germinate they should be uncovered and put into a good light position. Keep the bottom layer moist, adding water when necessary.

When planting out remember to cover the peat pellet completely with soil.

Sowing in Peat Pots
You need: Peat pots
           Seed compost
           Water
           Shallow container or seed tray
           Peat
           Newspaper or paper towel
           Seeds

Method: 1. Moisten the seed compost.
2. Fill the peat pots almost to the rim.
3. Level the surface.
4. Sow the seeds according to the instructions and if the seeds are to be planted deeply push them into the compost, otherwise sow them on the surface and cover lightly with seed compost.
5. Prepare the seed tray (see Peat Pellets, above) and arrange the pots.
6. The pots will soak up moisture, so make sure the bottom layer is kept moist.

Aftercare
Aftercare is similar to that of any other seedling in a peat block

or Jiffy pot, but when planting out remove the top rim of the peat pot. Any part of it left above the surface of the soil will act as a wick and draw moisture up and away from the plant.

Spacing Seeds

One way of coping with the problem of spacing seeds in a pot is to use margarine pots with lids. One lid can be used to press the compost, the other to space the seeds.

You need: Plastic margarine pots and two lids
Seeds and seed compost
Water

The pots and lids can be prepared beforehand; cut drainage holes in the pots, and cut or punch 3 or 4 holes evenly spaced round one lid, about 2 cm (¾ in) in from the edge.

Method: 1. Check that the seed compost is moist enough, and if not, add more water.
2. Fill the pots with compost level with the top.
3. Put on the plain lid – this light pressure is just enough to firm the compost.
4. Put on the lid with holes, and pop single seeds through the holes, or sprinkle fine seed into the holes. With shaky hands, the seeds can be scattered on top of the lid and brushed into the holes.
5. Add a little compost into the holes.
6. Take off the lid.

The pots can be watered and covered in the usual way, brought into full light when the seedlings show through, etc.

Week One

Onion Sets, Big Seeds and Ornamental Grasses

Onion Sets

Onion sets are partly grown onion bulbs which get off to a better start than seeds when planted in the spring. The best ones to buy are firm and up to 2 cm (¾ in) in diameter. Larger ones are liable to go to seed rather than forming onions.

Method:
1. In the garden, rake the soil and firm it.
2. Plant the onion sets in rows 25 cm (10 ins) apart. Push the bulbs into the ground so that only the pointed end is showing and plant them 7–10 cm (3–4 ins) apart.
3. Firm the soil round the sets because birds love to pull them out of the ground.

Big Seeds – Beetroot and Peas

Beetroot has big seeds which are really a cluster of seeds. They can be sown into seed-blocks etc. individually for later planting out, or planted directly into open ground, raised beds or

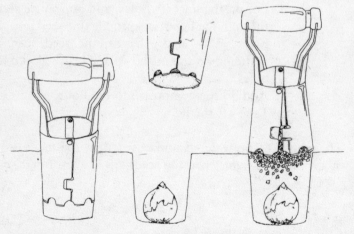

A bulb planter will also make holes for planting out seed blocks. This one, by Wolf Tools, has a push-in release device.

containers. Choose the varieties 'Boltardy' or 'Crimson Globe'.

Sow the seeds 2 cm (¾ ins) deep at intervals of 10 cm (4 ins) in rows 18 cm (7 ins) apart.

Aftercare
Water well once a week.

Peas: It is too early to plant either French or runner beans, but peas can be sown now. Choose 'Kelvedon Wonder' or 'Little Marvel'.

Plant peas in a triple row which measures 22 cm (9 ins) across, with 11 cm (4½ ins) between seeds and at a planting depth of 2.5–4 cm (1–1½ ins). The distance between rows should be 45 cm.

Aftercare
Once the plants are established, do not start to water until they are in flower. Then water well and never allow the plants to dry out. Regular picking of the pods encourages more to develop.

Ornamental Grasses
Sow the seeds of ornamental grasses in peat blocks or pots and grow them outside in a seed tray or cold frame to be planted out at a later stage. As mentioned on page 52, this prevents them from being mistaken for weeds.

Week Two
Small Seeds – Bush Tomatoes and Herbs

Growing Tomatoes
Dwarf and bush tomatoes need no staking or pinching out of shoots, and produce masses of small sweet tomatoes. There is nothing complicated about growing them and they grow indoors or in the garden, in any kind of container or in ordinary soil. They are not easily obtained as plants, so sow the seeds in April and grow them indoors on a sunny windowsill until the plants can be put outside in early June.

The seeds can be sown in peat blocks, Jiffy 7s or in peat or plastic pots filled with seed compost. Research has shown that sowing (and growing on) two or three seeds together will not affect the total yield or fruit with this kind of tomato, so there is no need to thin the seedlings.

To grow in a pot on the windowsill, or outside in a window-box or container, choose the varieties: Sub-Arctic Cherry, Pixie or Tiny Tim.

To grow in containers on a patio, raised beds or in a border, choose: Sigmabush or Sleaford Abundance.

You need: Peat blocks, Jiffy 7s or pots filled with seed compost
Seed tray
Tomato seeds (see above for varieties)
Water
Drainage tray

Method: 1. Make up the seed blocks, soak the Jiffy 7s or arrange the pots in the seed tray.
2. Put two seeds in the centre of each pot.
3. Push a little of the compost over the seed.
4. Water gently or mist spray.
5. Place on the drainage tray in a warm place, covering with plastic.

Aftercare

When the seedlings appear remove the plastic and place the tray on a sunny windowsill. Water when necessary.

Transplant into 12 cm (5 in) pots filled with a good soil-less compost, e.g. Levington's Potting Compost. Plant out in June or if they are to be grown indoors, into larger 20 cm (8 in) pots.

There should be enough fertiliser in the compost to last until the first flowers appear. After that, feed regularly with a tomato fertiliser and water when necessary.

Grow in a sunny spot – fruiting vegetables (like tomatoes and marrows) or rooting ones (like carrots, potatoes and beetroot) need plenty of sun to build up their food storing parts.

Growing Herbs

Herbs are very satisfying things to grow in small spaces because they are useful, scented, and have attractive leaf-shapes. A few pots of herbs on the windowsill, or by a path outside the kitchen door, make it easy to snip off sprigs for cooking. The ideal spot for herbs is sunny and well-drained, as many of these aromatic plants originate in Mediterranean countries. A raised bed suits them well, or they can be grown in any kind of container and in hanging baskets or individual pots.

Quite a lot of herbs are perennials, so growing them from cuttings, or with some rooted bits from an established plant, will give quicker results than growing them from seed.

Grow *parsley, pot marjoram, thyme, basil* and *chives* in pots on the windowsill or in a container or growing bag near the kitchen door. *Sage* is not a very good pot plant, so grow it in a larger container or garden border.

Mint, which spreads quickly, is best grown in a container on its own, or in a deep pot, bottomless bucket or drain pipe sunk in the soil in a shady place.

Lemon balm, fennel, angelica and *tarragon* are tall and look best in a border.

Rosemary makes a decorative shrub and a small bay tree will grow in a pot.

Sow seeds	Take cuttings	Divide plants
Parsley	Sage	Chives
Dill	Marjoram	Thyme
Fennel	Thyme	Mint
Thyme	Rosemary	Tarragon
Basil (indoors)	Bay	Lemon balm
Marjoram		

NOTE: *Parsley* is slow to germinate – it sometimes helps to pour boiling water over the soil before sowing. It is a biennial, but may not survive the winter, so it is usually sown every year.
Angelica is a biennial, best sown in June.
Basil is half-hardy and should be sown indoors. It does not dry very well, but sprigs can be used to flavour wine vinegar.

Later: Herbs should be picked before the plant flowers. They can be used fresh or dried and stored in jars (see July Weeks Two and Three), but some people prefer to freeze them. Wash, chop and fast-freeze them on a baking tray before packing into small containers to keep in the freezer until required.

Week Three
Sowing Annuals and Everlasting Flowers

Hardy Annuals

Here are some hardy annuals which are easy to grow. They can be sown outdoors in April in the positions where they are to flower. If you have difficulty in spacing the seeds, try pelleted seeds, seed strips, seed sticks or fluid sowing (see page 91). Alternatively, they can be sown in small pots or seed blocks, grown in a stand-by bed and planted out when they are big enough to have some recognisable leaves.

Nasturtiums and Californian Poppies flower best in poor rather dry soil. In rich soil, nasturtiums grow lots of leaves and very few flowers – which is why they are not suitable for growing with other plants in hanging baskets or containers.

Virginian stock is very useful – it gives quick results, flowering about a month after sowing. It can be sown any time from March to late July. For fun-growing, scratch a big initial about 40–50 cm long in the ground and sow Virginian stock seeds in the scratch-mark.

There are many more annuals to choose from. These are just a few, chosen because they are especially colourful, are good for flower-arranging, or have seedheads which can be dried:

Californian Poppy (Eschscholzia)	Marigold (Calendula)
Candytuft (Iberis)	Nasturtium
Cornflower (Centaurea)	Poppy
Gypsophila	Virginian Stock
Love-in-a-mist (Nigella)	

Half-hardy Annuals

Half-hardy annuals are more tender than hardy annuals and need to be sown indoors (or in a greenhouse) and planted out when all danger of frost is over. The seeds may be sown by any of the techniques given in the preceding notes and grown on for planting out in June. Grow only a few; they can take up a lot of space indoors if you are too ambitious. Half-hardy annuals can

be chosen from seed catalogues and instructions will be found
on the seed packets.

NOTE: Half-hardy plants which have to be planted very early
and need a lot of care, such as petunias, are best purchased as
young plants at the end of May or beginning of June.

Hint for a long-flowering season – nip off dead flowers so
that the plant will go on producing new buds. With annuals,
after the plant produces seed it dies.

Everlasting Flowers
Sow the seeds of everlasting flowers in April. They can be
planted directly into the garden, or sown into peat blocks, etc.,
and grown outside for planting out later.

Helichrysum (strawflower)
Acroclinium (also known as Helipterum)
Rhodanthe
These three all have crisp everlasting flowers which keep their
colour well.

Gypsophila dries easily
Nigella (love-in-a-mist) is sown for its pretty seed pods

Though the following plants are half-hardy, their seeds can be
sown out of doors in April:
Statice
Molucella (Bells of Ireland)

Lunaria (Honesty) is a hardy biennial grown for its seed pods
which do not develop until the second year.

Hardy perennials suitable for drying include:
Echinops (Globe Thistle)
Eryngium
Catananche
Achillea

NOTE: Some firms sell special packets of mixed seeds for
            everlasting flowers.

Week Four
Sowing Vegetable Seeds

Selection of Crops
The suggestions given here are intended for small-scale growing to give an introduction to the pleasures of gardening rather than a complete guide, and all the vegetables chosen could be grown in containers if necessary. Hence there is no mention of double digging, manuring or crop rotation. Brussels sprouts and leeks are not suitable for these conditions, but many other vegetables can be grown with success. The main thing is to get started, and to choose things which are simple to grow. These are satisfying because they give good results. The practical problems have been considered carefully whilst trying to offer a variety and the following range of vegetables has been chosen: Beetroot, carrots, lettuce, peas, radishes, spring onions.

Sowing Vegetable Seeds Outdoors
You need:　Outdoor bed, prepared last month
　　　　　　Rake
　　　　　　Stick or hoe
　　　　　　Garden line (a piece of strong string and two sticks will do)
　　　　　　Water
　　　　　　Seeds
　　　　　　Labels, or sticks and small plastic bags and twist ties

Seed sowing out of doors. Raking and firming the soil.

Method: 1. Make a plan, deciding and marking where the rows will be. Instructions on the seed packet will give row spacing and depth of planting.

Vegetables do best in a place which gets plenty of sun, so do not plant in the shade or plan to grow tall things where they will shadow the rest.

2. Rake the soil to make a fine surface that is level.
3. Firm the soil by treading, shuffling the feet along where the rows are planned.
4. With a garden line for guidance, draw a line with a stick or corner of a hoe to the right depth for the type of seed.
5. Water along this line.
6. Sow the seed thinly. (See pages 42–45 and 90–95).
7. With the back of the rake, draw the soil from the sides of the drill over the seeds and firm lightly, or cover the seeds with sieved compost to prevent surface-hardening.
8. Mark the rows with a label, or place the seed packet over a stick, covering it with a small plastic bag held with a wire twist.

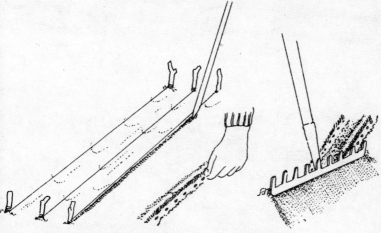

Making a drill, sowing the seeds and covering them.

May

Week One
Sowing Large Seeds in Pots

You need: Seeds of: Ornamental Gourds
Sunflowers
Courgettes
Nasturtiums

Plant pots, plastic cups with drainage
holes (4 each)
Seed compost – already moist
Compost presser
4 labels and waterproof pen

*For each
person*

Plastic tray
Capillary matting to fit tray
Water

Method: 1. Fill one pot with seed compost.
2. Firm down gently with presser.
3. Push 2 gourd seeds into compost (flat seeds are planted vertically, not 'lying down', 1–2 cm deep ($\frac{1}{2}$–$\frac{3}{4}$ in).
4. Label (name of seed and of gardener).
5. Arrange pots on capillary matting placed in tray.

Repeat for the other seeds using the rest of the pots. Water the capillary matting. Grow in a good light and do not let the matting dry out. If two seeds germinate, cut off the weaker seedling with scissors. When the second pair of leaves show, water with diluted fertiliser. Plant out of doors at the beginning of June.

Ornamental Gourds: Plant in rich soil, against a trellis or with supporting strings.

Sunflowers: Medium soil, against a wall or fence

Nasturtiums: Poor soil

Courgettes: Rich soil, on a mound. Water well in summer.

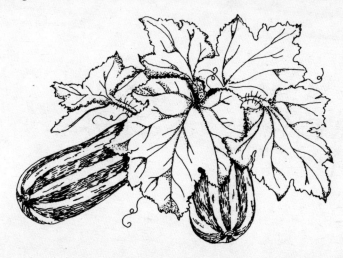

Week Two
Pricking Out and Planting Out

Pricking Out

You may have used seed-blocks, etc., for sowing seeds, in which case there is no need for pricking out. Seedlings which have grown from a scattering of seed sown in pots or seed trays need to be spaced out so that they have more room to grow. They are ready for transplanting when they are large enough to pick up by the first pair of leaves and the second pair (the 'true' leaves) have developed. A damp piece of newspaper or paper towel keeps the seedlings fresh whilst you work.

You need: Pots or seed tray of seedlings
Fresh pots and seed trays
Seed compost (peat based or John Innes no. 1)
Old fork or spoon
Dibber
Newspaper or paper towel
Water
Watering can with fine spray, misting bottle or a deep dish for watering
Labels

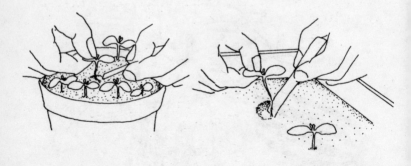

Method: 1. Water the seedlings.
2. Moisten the seed compost if necessary.
3. Fill the pots or seed tray, as for seed sowing.
4. Wet a folded piece of newspaper or paper towel.
5. Dig into the tray of seedlings with the fork or spoon and transfer a clump of them onto the damp paper.
6. The seedlings should be planted about 5 cm (2 ins) apart in the pot or tray. You can make holes one at a time with the dibber or spaced with a home-made or proprietary multiple-dibber.
7. Prise the seedlings apart gently, handling them by one of the first pair of leaves, never by the stem.
8. Gently place each one into a hole, firming the compost round it so that there are no air pockets.
9. Label.
10. Water sparingly with a very fine spray or soak the seed tray for 5–10 minutes in the sink and then drain.

Aftercare

The seedlings need plenty of light and sun, a compost that is moist but not over-wet, and liquid fertiliser once a week until they are large enough to plant out.

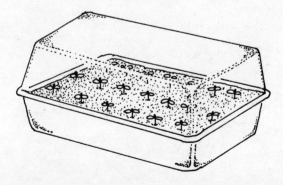

Planting Out

Some of the plants which have been grown in Jiffy pots, etc., such as ornamental grasses, vegetables or hardy annuals, should now be planted out in their final growing positions.

The ground should be dug over and large stones removed (small ones do not matter). Fertilise as recommended and rake level. If you are planting in rows you will need a garden line (stout twine stretched between two pegs), a straight stick or a plank. One useful aid is a measuring stick, the width of the bed, marked at intervals with notches or round-headed screws. This is especially useful to those who are visually handicapped. Alternatively, a short measuring stick could be cut to the length of the required distance between the plants, or the spaces can be measured by using hand spans or the length of a trowel.

Planting out peat blocks or peat pots is simple as they can be placed directly in holes in the ground. Plants in plastic pots need to be watered before removal. Some flimsy plastic or polystyrene pots can be torn away. Some disabled people find difficulty in removing plants from pots. Normal practice is to splay the fingers of one hand over the surface of the compost, thus supporting the plant, and turning the pot upside down. If the plant does not fall out of the pot easily, squeeze the sides of

the pot and gently ease out the plant. Alternatively, you may need to give the pot a smart tap on the bottom.

You need: A garden line, stick or plank
                Trowel or bulb planter
                Plants
                Water in a bucket
                An empty can or cup

Method: 1. Position the row marker.
             2. Dig a hole with the trowel or use the bulb planter to lift out the soil for the first plant.
             3. Pour a can of water into the hole.
             4. Put in the plant so that it sits a little lower than the level of the soil.
             5. Draw the soil over the top. This prevents the peat or potting compost acting as a wick and drying out the plant.

Aftercare

If the plants wilt, water when necessary until they are established. Newspaper will temporarily shade the plants from hot sun and prevent wilting.

Stages in planting out. Pour water into the planting hole, insert the plant and carefully cover the surface.

Week Three
Hanging Baskets

Many kinds of hanging basket are now available. The plastic ones are easiest to fill, and some of these are designed with a built-in drip saucer so that they can be used indoors or out. The conventional kind of hanging basket is made of wire and lined with a thick layer of sphagnum moss. Apart from the difficulty or expense of obtaining moss, it needs practice to line the basket efficiently and the whole operation can be very messy! It is much better to line a wire basket with black or dark green plastic sheeting, or (more expensively) with a strong plastic mesh which can be bought for the purpose.

Drainage material is not necessary in a hanging basket; it dries out all too quickly anyway. But a useful hint is to use some crumbled Oasis (from the remains of flower arranging) at the bottom. This keeps moist while surplus water drains away.

A small hanging basket can be used for a single plant, preferably something trailing. Ivy, tradescantia or plectranthus (Swedish ivy) are good for indoors. For a basket in a window or out of doors choose a flowering plant, such as ivy-leaved geranium or trailing begonia.

Larger hanging baskets can be planted with a mixture of plants, depending on what effect is required.

You need: A hanging basket
Plastic lining if necessary
A sharp pointed tool for punching holes
Potting compost
Plants (bought or raised from seeds or cuttings)
Water

Method: 1. Line the basket if necessary. The plastic can be punched with four or five holes beforehand, or this can be done after planting.
2. Check that the compost is moist enough. If not, add more water and mix.
3. Half-fill the basket with compost.
4. Decide where the plants are to go; take them out of their pots or plant trays and place them in position. Work from the centre to the rim adding compost round the plants.
5. Fill the basket to within 2.5 cm (1 in) of the top to allow for watering.
6. Check that drainage holes have been punched.
7. Water the basket using a watering can with a fine rose, and drain.

Aftercare
Indoor plants can be hung up straight away, but outdoor baskets need to be placed somewhere light and sheltered, but not in full sun, for at least a week before hanging up. A cold frame is a good place. Water regularly – never let the basket dry out. After the first four weeks give a liquid feed and then feed weekly for the rest of the season.

Hanging basket alternatives
Homemade hanging baskets can be made from all kinds of things – colanders, small plastic buckets, ice cream containers or washing up bowls with drainage holes, or ordinary plant pots in suspended bowls or baskets. Attractive macramé holders can be bought or home made. A pulley fixed to the bracket will allow the basket to be lowered for watering.

Week Four
Preparing Outdoor Containers .

Growing plants in containers makes it possible to have a mini-garden almost anywhere – on a balcony, a roof-top, or any small paved area. The essentials are good drainage, good compost, careful watering to avoid drying out in the summer, and regular feeding of the plants with fertiliser.

One advantage of container growing is that the soil can be chosen to suit the plant – a peaty lime-free soil for azaleas and heathers for instance, and poor sandy soil for nasturtiums.

When planting new containers, check that they have good drainage holes, and that drainage will not be impeded by standing on a flat surface. Some containers already have a rim at the base, or have legs or casters, but others may need to be raised. Windowboxes need to be supported clear of the sills.

If preparing containers which have already been used for spring-flowering plants, dig out the bulbs and plants. Primulas and pansies may be planted in a shady or semi-shady part of the garden or potted separately and kept in a shady place. The leaves of bulbs should be allowed to shrivel and then the bulbs may be dried for a few days in the sun before being stored in a cool dry place.

Large containers do not need to be emptied – just take some of the soil from the top. Loosen the remaining soil and stir in some fertiliser (amount according to the size of the container). Top up with fresh potting compost.

Large containers to be freshly prepared can be filled with a mixture of equal parts of soil, peat and coarse sand (or perlite) with the addition of some granular fertiliser (the amount depending on the size of the container).

To prepare containers
You need: Drainage material
Potting compost (soil-less or John Innes no. 2) or soil mixture (see above)
Trowel
Water

Method: 1. Put a layer of drainage material at the bottom of the container.
   2. Fill to the top with potting compost or soil mixture.
   3. Water.

Let the soil in the container settle for a week before planting.

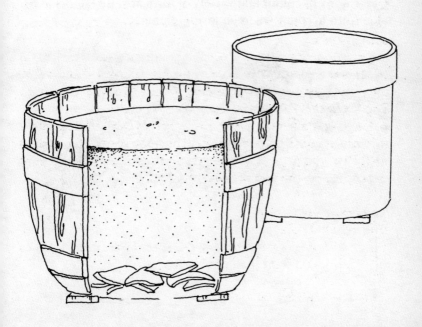

June

Week One
Planting Outdoor Containers

Outdoor containers may be planted with all kinds of plants and the choice depends on whether they are in the sun or in the shade.

Annuals, both hardy and half-hardy, chosen to give a profusion of flowers over a long period, will need no other attention than watering, fertilising and dead-heading.

There are many perennial plants which provide attractive flowers or foliage, such as geraniums, fuchsias, ivies and herbs. Shrubs or small trees make permanent features.

In a sunny spot, vegetables may be grown and lettuces will do well in a shady spot if they are well watered.

Harmony of colour and variety of form are also factors to be taken into account when choosing plants.

Planting

You need: Outdoor container, ready prepared (see May Week Four)
Plants
Trowel

Method: 1. Plant taller plants in the centre.
2. Plant trailing plants at the edges.
3. Water.
4. Shade with a newspaper for the first two or three days if the sun is hot.

Some Plants to Choose:

Upright Plants

Geraniums (zonal or regal)
Begonias (tuberous and fibrous)
Fuchsias
Petunias
Chlorophytum (spider plant)

Trailing Plants

Petunias (cascade)
Geraniums (ivy leafed)
Lobelia
Tradescantia
Hedera (ivy)

Grow These in the Sun

Ageratum
Alyssum
Antirrhinum (snapdragon)
Calendula (pot marigold)
Geranium (zonal)
Lobelia
Nasturtium
Petunia

Grow These in Partial Shade

Clarkia
Fuchsia
Hydrangea
Impatiens (busy lizzie)
Myosotis (forget-me-not)
Nemesia
Nicotiana (tobacco plant)
Pansy

These Will Grow in Shade

Ferns
Fatsia japonica
Hedera (ivy)
Vinca (periwinkle)

Week Two
Planting Out Half-Hardy Annuals and Vegetables

Half-hardy annuals and the large seeds which have been grown in pots, seed blocks, etc., can be planted out now. Some large seeds, such as sunflowers, marrows, ornamental gourds, runner beans and French beans can be sown directly into the soil if they have not been started already in pots. The sowing distances are the same as for planting out. Good rich soil in a sunny position and liberal watering are needed for all these plants.

Half-hardy annuals
Follow the instructions on the seed packet.

Sunflowers
Sunflowers can be planted out or sown directly in a really sunny spot – they like plenty of room to grow so plant them at least 60 cm (2 ft) apart. Water them well throughout the summer as they grow fast. Provide some support such as a tall

stick, or grow them near a wall or fence to which they can be tied, otherwise they may be blown over in a storm.

A sunflower race is fun. Set a judging date at the end of the summer and see which has grown the tallest. Another idea is to measure them week by week and make a chart of growth. At the end of the season when the seeds have ripened, the sunflower heads can be picked and saved to hang up for the birds in winter. A few of the seeds can be reserved for planting next year.

Marrows and Pumpkins
Weighing and measuring the girth of marrows and pumpkins is another fun-activity. Bush marrows, which take up less space than trailing marrows, should be planted 60 cm (2 ft) apart.

Courgettes
These are marrows which are eaten when they are very small. Cut courgettes as soon as the withered flower falls, when they are 10–15 cm (4–6 ins) long.

Ornamental Gourds
Plant these about 1.5–2 metres apart (4–6 ft) and train them up sticks or a trellis.

Runner Beans
Strong supports are needed for runner beans and they can be grown to make a 'wig-wam'. Plant them on the north side of the vegetable patch or they will shadow other plants. Plant them 30 cm (1 ft) apart. Pick the beans regularly. Have a competition to grow the longest pod.

Week Three
Flower Arranging

There are two main types of plastic foam used to hold stems in flower arranging. One will soak up water and is used for fresh flowers. It can also be used dry for arranging dried flowers and grasses, particularly those with fragile stems. But there is a harder, crisper sort of foam which is better for dried material with woody stems, or for flowers, leaves or cones which have been mounted on wires.

Both kinds of foam can be bought in a variety of shops. The cheapest way is to buy brick-shaped blocks which can be cut to the shape needed with a knife (not necessarily a very sharp one, a table knife will do). Florists and garden shops stock Oasis, Florapak and other makes of floral foam, together with holders of various kinds. Shallow plastic dishes with spikes to hold the Oasis firmly in place are not expensive, and can be used again and again, renewing the Oasis when necessary.

Avoid tall vases – they are difficult for beginners to arrange and can be very unstable – otherwise you can make use of all kinds of container. Pie dishes, margarine pots, pilchard tins, coffee mugs – almost anything will do.

To Make a Fresh Flower Arrangement

You need: A container that will hold water
Oasis or other (wet) foam
Rubber bands or sticky tape
Flowers and leaves
Scissors, flower snips or secateurs
Water

Method: 1. Soak the Oasis in water for at least one hour.
2. Cut the block of Oasis to suit the container. It should stand about 3–5 cm (1½–2 ins) higher than the rim of the container.
3. Make sure you have left a space for topping up the water level in the container.
4. Wedge the Oasis in place holding it firmly with rubber bands or sticky tape if necessary.

5. Outline the shape of the arrangement with the thinnest, most pointed material. Place a round shape, the biggest flower, towards the centre of the arrangement, cutting the stem quite short. Arrange the middle-sized material with stems of varying lengths as if they radiate from this point.

6. The strongest colours should be towards the centre and the more delicate material to the outside.

7. Check that the Oasis is hidden; if not, add some extra leaves to cover it.

8. Pour some water into the container.

Aftercare

Top up the container with water when necessary.

Spraying with a fine mist of water every day will help to keep the flowers fresh.

Stages in flower arranging. Stand the bowl on non-slip matting to keep it steady while you work.

Week Four
Sowing for Next Year – Biennials and Perennials

More sowing of seeds can be done in June, with biennial and perennial plants which will flower next year. Using the same techniques as given in the April notes (page 90), the following seeds can be sown, transplanting into flowering positions at a later date:

Pansies	Violas
Angelica (herb)	Primulas
Forget-me-nots	Wallflowers
Stocks	Honesty
Foxgloves	Sweet Williams
Antirrhinums (Snapdragons)	Dianthus (Pinks)

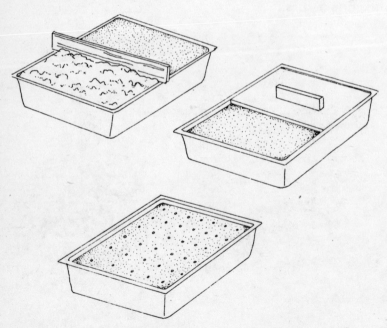

Seed sowing in trays. Levelling off the compost, lightly pressing it down and sowing the seed evenly.

NOTE: Another seed-sowing session could take place during August. Hardy annuals which are sown then will flower earlier than those sown in the spring.

Suitable seeds

Calendula (pot marigold)   Candytuft
Clarkia   Godetia
Gypsophila   Linum (flax)
Larkspur

Using a coathanger to support a plastic bag over a seed tray.

Pots of seedlings can be stood on the windowsill until they are large enough for planting out.

Week Five
Pressing Flowers and Collecting Grasses

Pressing Flowers

You need: Flowers, grasses, leaves
An old telephone book, or discarded thick book with absorbent pages
Blotting paper, sheets cut slightly smaller than the pages of the books

Method: 1. Gather plant material on a dry day and press straight away. If it is necessary to pick flowers the day before, stand them in water overnight and cut off the wet part of stem before pressing.
2. Open the book flat and lay a sheet of blotting paper on one page. Space out flowers, leaves and grasses on it, arranging petals and leaves attractively; then gently cover with another sheet of blotting paper.
3. Carefully close the book.
4. Repeat as required, opening the book at another page.

Pressing flowers – to prepare for making pressed flower pictures (see November Week Three).

5. Place heavy objects on the closed book, and leave for three or four weeks or longer until completely dry. Keep the pressed material in the book until required for picture making.

NOTE: Discard thick stalks before pressing, and press the petals of roses separately – flowers can be reassembled after pressing. Flowers with thick centres – like daisies – can be flattened with the thumb before being arranged on the blotting paper – inspect these during pressing, and renew the blotting paper if damp.

Clematis, pansies, buttercups and delphiniums are very successful, and delphiniums in particular keep their colour well. A variety of shapes and colours helps in making interesting dried-flower pictures, so be adventurous. Press silver leaves such as senecio maritima, small blackberry leaves, and delicate flowers and grasses. Include wild flowers – especially Meadowsweet and Cow parsley. Press some curled tendrils from Sweet peas or Clematis, and some fine stems – These may be needed to give the finishing touches to a picture.

Ferns remain more flexible if they are brushed lightly with cooking oil before pressing.

Collecting Grasses

Dried grasses are useful in craft work as well as flower arrangements. Wild grasses and cereals such as oats, wheat and barley may be dried, as well as the ornamental grasses from the garden. Cut them whilst still green, before they flower – that is, just as the stamens appear at the bottom of the flower spike. Watching the development of grasses is interesting – most people do not think of them as flowers. Collect grasses on a dry day and do not try to strip the leaves before drying – this is easier to do afterwards. Dry them in a warm airy place out of the sun for 1–2 weeks.

Grasses with a single spike should be tied in small bunches and hung upside down. (see July Week Two).

Grasses with loose arching sprays dry best in an empty vase.

Grasses which are very delicate can be dried flat on box lids or paper-lined trays.

July

Week One
Lavender Sticks

Lavender is ready for picking when the buds show some colour but the flowers are not yet open. The stems are most pliable if picked two days before they are to be used. Freshly picked they sometimes snap and if kept longer they become brittle.

For each stick
you need: 7 or 9 stems of lavender, 30 cm (12 ins) long (it is important to have an odd number of stems)
Ribbon, no more than 1.2 cm (½ in) wide, one piece 30 cm (12 ins) long and one 22 cm (9 ins) long
Scissors

Method: 1. Strip the stems of leaves and buds below the flower head (these trimmings can be spread on paper and dried to use in pot-pourri – see note below).
2. Tie the lavender together just beneath the flowers with one end of the longest ribbon.
3. Turn it upside down, and bend the stems over the flowers.
4. Weave the ribbon under and over the stems, keeping the ribbon flat and pulling firmly into a 'bottle' shape.
5. Continue weaving round and round to the end of the ribbon.
6. Wind the second piece of ribbon round at this point and finish with a bow.
7. Trim off the ends of the lavender stems as shown opposite.

Alternative

To give a fatter 'bottle', an odd number of *paired* stems can be used (i.e. using 14 or 18 lavender stems).

NOTE 1:   This is the time to cut lavender for drying, for use in lavender bags later. Stand the stems in a vase (with no water) in a warm room, or hang in small bunches, or spread out to dry on paper. When dry, the lavender can be stripped from the stems. The dried leaves are also fragrant, and can be used in potpourri.

NOTE 2:   Some preparatory work may be needed to explain 'weaving'. This can be practised using ribbon and drinking straws.

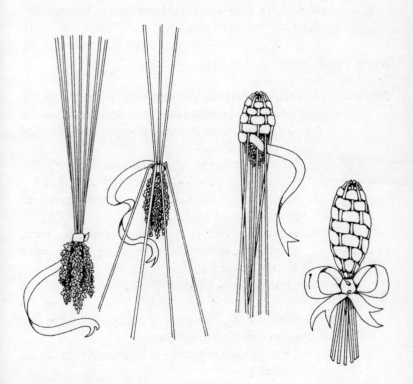

Week Two
Pot Pourri and Dried Herbs (1)

Pot pourri is a mixture of dried petals and spices which is kept in a jar or used in sachets for its perfume. Scented leaves and herbs can be added – and there are many different mixtures which can be used, with fixatives and perfume oils to give a long-lasting result. Consequently 'pot pourri' is often used to describe a medley of things; in fact, it literally means 'rotten pot'. There are two main kinds of pot pourri, moist and dry, and traditionally the basis for the moist one is made by layering half-dried rose petals with salt in a sealed pot for a few weeks. This 'rotted' stuff is then dried, crumbled, and added to other ingredients before being used in bowls or jars to scent a room.

Modern recipes for moist pot pourri still include salt, though they are not fermented in the same way. The recipe here is for dry pot pourri, which can be used either in bowls or for making scented sachets.

Drying Petals
You need: Scented roses
Fragrant flowers such as pinks and some chosen to give colour, (e.g. marigolds, pansies, zinnias)
Trays or wire racks lined with paper towels

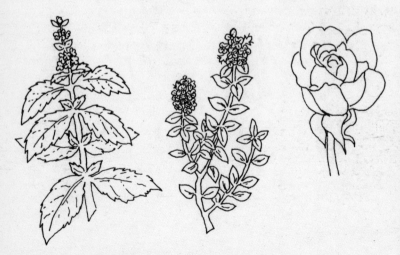

Method: 1. Gather fully open flowers on a dry day after the morning dew has dried. Don't use dying flowers, or fallen petals.
2. Pick the petals from the flowers.
3. Spread them on the lined trays.
4. Leave them in a dark airy place for 4–5 days, stirring the petals daily until thoroughly dry.

Drying Leaves

You need: Sprays of leaves from lemon or rose-scented geraniums, lemon balm, lavender, verbena, thyme, mint, rosemary, sage, etc., as available
String or rubber bands
Small luggage-labels and pen

Method: 1. Identify the different leaves and scents.
2. Tie small bunches of scented leaves or herbs together and label them.
3. Hang the bunches to dry in an airy place until the leaves are crisp.

NOTE: A large number of bunches can be hung on a line, or on wire coathangers.

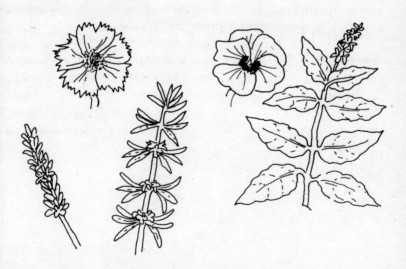

Week Three
Pot Pourri and Dried Herbs (2)

This uses the petals and leaves which were prepared last week.

To Make Pot Pourri
You need: 2 large handfuls of rose petals
2 large handfuls of other flowers and dried scented leaves and herbs
50 gm or 2 oz ground orris root
50 gm or 2 oz ground coriander
15 gm or ½ oz ground cinnamon
A wide necked jar and lid (such as a glass or plastic sweet jar)

Method: 1. Strip the leaves from the stems and crumble them.
2. Put the petals and crumbled leaves in the jar.
3. Add the orris root (which 'fixes' the scent).
4. Add the rest of the spices and shake well.
5. Put the lid on the jar and leave it for about a month.

The pot pourri can then be used for making sachets, or simply kept in a decorative bowl or jar for fragrance.

Dried Herbs   Taking each bunch separately, the dried leaves can be stripped from the stalks and crumbled, and then stored in labelled screw-topped jars.

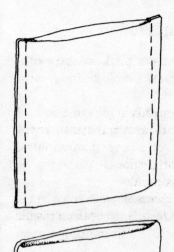

1. Fold a strip of material and sew down the sides.

2. Fold the top over.

3. Turn the bag inside out and run a line of stitches round.

4. Fill the bag and draw up the thread. Tie firmly.

5. Finish with a ribbon bow if desired.

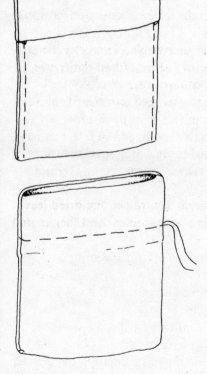

Bags for pot pourri and lavender can be made quite simply from odds and ends of material, following the diagrams on this page.

Week Four
Preserving Leaves and Drying Flowers

To provide plenty of material for craft work in the winter months, it is necessary to learn a few simple techniques of drying and preserving.

Flowers and seed heads will not be ready at the same time, of course. Collecting suitable material at the best time for preserving it is an activity which can spread over many months, from drying pussy-willow catkins in the spring to gathering the last of the seed pods in late autumn.

About now the everlasting flowers which were sown in the spring will be ready, and there are many plants, both cultivated and wild, which will provide interesting and useful material.

Preserving Leaves

Leaves which are mature – not young soft growth – can be preserved in a solution of equal parts of water and glycerine (or 2 parts water to 1 part glycerine) or undiluted antifreeze, or equal parts of antifreeze and water.

Evergreen leaves can be preserved at any time of the year, but take up the solution best in the months of growth.

Choose leaves which are healthy and free from insect damage. Cut off any damaged leaves, or leaves which spoil the shape of a spray, so that you do not waste the preserving solution.

Suitable foliage: beech, berberis, holly, oak, mahonia.
NOTE: Ferns and ivy leaves can be soaked in the solution until they change colour.

Cupressus dries naturally without glycerine.

Method: 1. Use boiling water and add to the glycerine.
2. Leave to get cold.
3. Fill a jar to a depth of 5–7 cm (2–3 ins).
4. Crush the ends of the stems,
5. Keep the stems in the solution, topping up when necessary, until the leaves are supple and glistening. This takes a varying length of time,

depending on the type of leaf – e.g. Holly takes about 4 days, Beech 3–4 weeks.

Drying Flowers
Pick before the flowers are fully open, for they will continue to open whilst drying.

Strip the leaves. Hang in small bunches, upside down in a dark dry place.

Flowers to use:

Acroclinium	Astilbe
Achillea	Stachys lanata
Amaranthus	Statice sinuata

Echinops and Eringium: pick when young and spray with clear lacquer

Hydrangea: pick flowers that are just beginning to change colour and get dry. Stand the stems in a jar with 2 cm (about an inch) of water and leave until all the water has disappeared.

Helichrysum (Strawflower)
Harvest the flowers when they are just opening the outer ring of petals and the centre is closed tight. As they dry the flowers continue to open. Harvesting later means that they will open too much. The stems are very brittle when dried and impractical to use in flower arranging, so the flowers can be picked with only a short length of stem. More buds will open later giving a succession of harvesting.

For most craft work the stems are not necessary, but if the flowers are to be used for flower arranging they need to be put on wires the same day. If this is not possible, they can be kept for a day or two in a plastic bag in the refrigerator. Flower heads for craft work can be spread on trays or cardboard box lids and dried thoroughly before being packed away in boxes and stored in a dry place.

To Wire Helichrysum Flowers
You need: A bundle of flower wires (No. 20) or lengths of a
           a wire which is firm but bendable
           Helichrysum heads
           Pair of pliers
           Tin or jar filled with dry sand

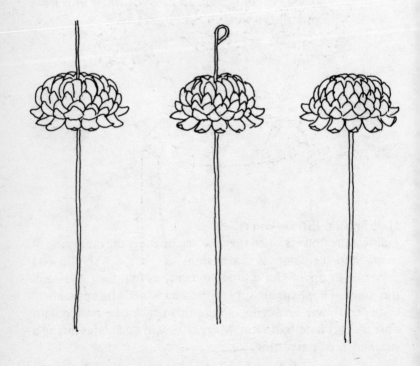

Method: 1. From the back push the end of a wire through the centre of a flower until it projects 3–5 cm (1–2 ins). This can be done very neatly by pushing the wire through the stem but accuracy is not essential.
2. Bend the wire over to make a hook shape.
3. Pull the wire back so that the hook is embedded in the flower.
4. Stand the flower in the jar of sand by its 'wired stem'.
5. Leave until thoroughly dry (about a week).

Afterwards

Projecting stems can be broken off or neatened by binding round the stem and wire with florist's tape.

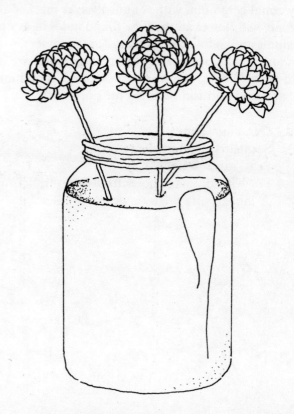

August

Week One
Taking Geranium Cuttings

The thick stems of geraniums are sturdy to handle and yet easy to cut. Cuttings root most readily in July, August and September, but can also be taken in March when pruning back overwintered plants. Geraniums (more accurately known as pelargoniums) are zonal, ivy-leafed, regal or scented. The ordinary zonal geranium, with rounded leaves marked with a darker zone, will flower all the year round indoors. Ivy leafed pelargoniums are useful trailing plants for containers, window boxes and hanging baskets. The regal pelargoniums are showy but need greater care; the leaves of scented geraniums are delicately shaped and can be dried for pot-pourri.

You need: Geranium plants
Secateurs or sharp knife
Peat, sand, water
Pot with drainage holes to take several cuttings
A dibber, and a trowel or scoop

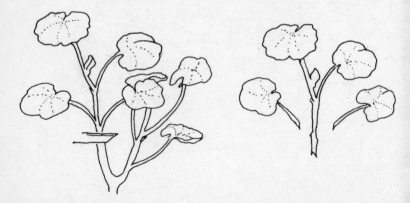

Method:
1. Choose stems which have joints close together, not long 'leggy' ones.
2. Cut cleanly 7.5–10 cm (3–4 ins) long, just below the leaf joint.
3. Leave a tidy 'mother plant' by cutting the stem again, just above the next leaf joint.
4. Pinch off any flower buds on the cutting.
5. Remove all leaves except the top two and the little bunch of new leaves at the tip.
6. Take as many cuttings as you need and let them lie on the bench whilst preparing the pots – this 'wilting' seems to improve the chances of successful rooting.
7. Mix up rooting compost of 1 part sand to 1 part peat (by volume) and moisten just sufficiently to hold together when squeezed.
8. Fill the pot with the compost and press lightly.
9. Using a dibber, make holes for the cuttings; about a third of the cutting should be in the compost. Firm them in.
10. Place the pot in bright light, but not in the sun at first, on a drainage tray or saucer. Do *not* cover in any way.

Aftercare

Water if necessary, but do not keep the compost soggy. Remove dead leaves or any cuttings that do not 'take'.

Week Two
A Miniature Garden

A miniature garden can give a lot of pleasure, particularly to people who cannot get out of doors. A meat or pie plate can be used – but the shallower the container the more attention is needed to grow the plants successfully. A tureen or roasting dish is deeper and will give better results. A seed tray sitting on a tray lined with capillary-matting will need less intense care over watering. Most miniature gardens benefit from a daily mist spray of water to prevent the plants from drying out.

If using a dish without drainage holes spread a layer of pebbles or charcoal (or both) in the dish before filling it with compost.

You need: A dish (see above)
Drainage material if necessary
Potting compost
Small plants
Stones or gravel
A mirror
Small figures, etc. (optional)
Planting tool

Method:
1. Put the pebbles or charcoal in the dish.
2. Fill with compost to within 2 cm (1 in) of the rim.
3. Make a little hill of compost to vary the level if desired. Choose the planting positions of the plants.
4. Dig holes with a table fork, small dibber or spoon. If the roots of the plant are deeper than the plate, dig a wider hole, shake the soil off the roots and spread them out.
5. Firm the plants into place – but gently – do not ram them in.
6. Add features such as a mirror pond with stones round the edges and little paths.

7. Spaces can be filled in with moss, sand or gravel.

Try to keep everything in proportion – flowers, small rockery plants and miniature trees – as well as any additions such as model bridges, garden seats or toy animals and people. Paths can be made from small stones, fine gravel or sand. Aquaria suppliers stock coloured gravel and suitable accessories.

Some Plants to Choose

Small conifers or 'bonsai' trees
Miniature ('fairy') roses
Saxifrage (cushion types)
Thyme (green, golden or variegated)
Mosses and small ferns
Miniature bulbs
Small varieties of sedum
Miniature varieties of pinks, linaria, etc.

Contrasting shapes, textures and colours look attractive, so choose the positions of plants carefully, placing variegated foliage against green, large leaves against small, and use rocks, pebbles, wood and pieces of bark to add texture.

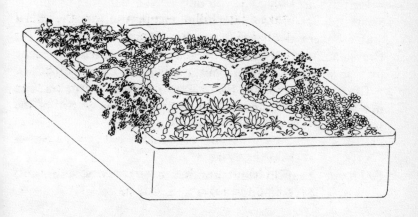

Week Three
Taking More Cuttings – Indoor Plants and Succulents

Indoor Plants

Taking more cuttings of indoor plants at this time will provide material for making a terrarium in September (see September Week Five) and for indoor plant arrangements in the winter.

Follow the instructions given in February Week Three.

Succulents

Cuttings of succulents will be needed for "A Succulent Dish Garden" (November Week Two).

Succulents are plants with fleshy leaves or stems which can store water. Cactus plants are really succulents and form a special group – but their spines make them difficult to handle. Some spines are hooked and extremely irritating if they get under the skin, and some are dangerously long and sharp. Some of the agave succulents have sharp saw-toothed leaves, so it would be best to choose from the following groups:

> Echeveria
> Crassula
> Sempervivum
> Sedum

Cuttings are very easy; you only need a leaf from the plant. Some echeverias or sempervivums (houseleeks) produce 'babies' themselves, which can be snapped off and planted. Crassula argentea (the Jade tree) can be propagated by a leaf or by a short stem cutting from the end of a "branch".

Christmas Cactus and Easter Cactus are also succulents, and new plants can be grown by breaking off one or two of the segments at the tips of the "branches".

You need: Leaf or stem cuttings
            Seed compost

Dry sand
Plastic pots
A dibber

Method: 1. Let the cuttings dry for a few days if possible.
2. Fill the pots with barely moist compost almost to the top.
3. Sprinkle sand over the surface of the compost.
4. Insert the cut end of a stem or leaf cutting, using the dibber.
5. Place in good light but not direct sun.
6. Do not water or cover.

Aftercare
Water only sparingly.

Week Four
Potting Up Geraniums

The geranium cuttings should be rooted by now – give one of them a little tug. If it resists, then roots have formed. Alternatively, there may be new leaves growing. Use John Innes no. 2 compost to allow fairly dry winter conditions – a peat-based compost is more difficult to wet again if it dries out.

You need: Pot of rooted cuttings
Newspaper or plastic
10 cm (4 in) pots (one for each cutting)
John Innes compost no. 2
Trowel or scoop
Water

Method: 1. Tip out the rooted cuttings onto newspaper or plastic, or gently dig them out of the pot.
2. Put some compost into each pot (about ⅓ full).
3. Holding a cutting centrally in a pot, add more compost, filling the pot to the top.
4. Firm the compost round the little plant, leaving about 1 cm (½ in) at the top of the pot for watering.
5. Water and leave to drain.

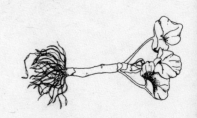

Aftercare

Keep in good light with a minimum winter temperature of 7°C (45°F) and water sparingly. In a warm place, more water will be needed. Start to fertilise with half-strength liquid feed at the end of February. Pinch out the growing tip when the plant is 15 cm (6 ins) high to encourage it to become bushy. Plant out at the end of May in a sunny position.

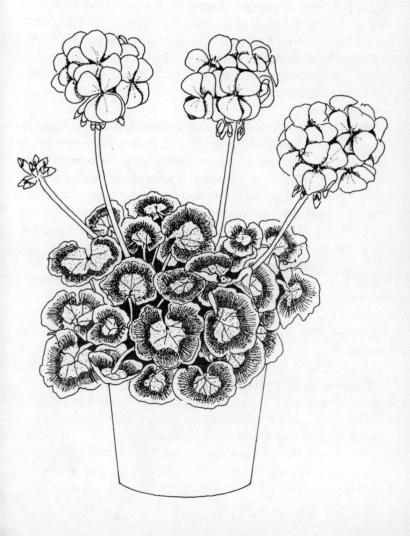

September

Notes on Bulbs

Bulbs are some of the easiest things to grow. Since the flower is already formed inside, success is almost guaranteed, at least for the first year. Compared with seeds, bulbs are easy to handle and to space out when planting. There is an enormous choice – bulbs can be chosen to grow indoors, outdoors, in frames or greenhouses, to flower in spring, summer, autumn or winter – so bulb planting can be an activity carried out at various times during the year.

It is important to follow a few simple rules in order to get the best results. Buy good sized bulbs, plant them as soon as possible after buying, don't let them dry out whilst growing, and when they have finished flowering, cut off only the flowerheads and let the leaves and stalks die down naturally to feed the bulb for the following year.

Growing bulbs indoors needs a little extra care. Spring-flowering bulbs, for instance, need a taste of winter before they will flower, so either buy 'prepared' bulbs or provide a spell of 'cold and dark' after planting. Prepared bulbs have been given a carefully calculated period in cold store – they cost a little more, but will flower early. Hyacinths are particularly responsive to this treatment. Untreated bulbs need about six weeks of cool, damp dark conditions before bringing into the light – wrapping the bowls in black polythene and standing them in a shaded part of the garden works quite well. Failing that, store in the coolest part of the house – and don't forget to water them when necessary or the roots will not develop properly and the flowers will be damaged.

To ensure flowering at the same time, choose bulbs of the same kind for each bowl – mixed planting can prove very disappointing as the bulbs seldom grow at an equal rate.

All kinds of interesting containers such as old soup tureens can be used to grow indoor bulbs, but they should be deep enough to allow for plenty of root growth and have pebbles, gravel or crocks (broken bits of old clay plant pots) at the bottom for drainage. Some bulbs will actually grow in water (see September, Week One) but others will not tolerate waterlogged roots.

When planting in a large bowl, it is a very good idea to plant one or two of the bulbs in a plant pot sunk into the bulb-fibre. The rest of the bulbs will develop roots around the pot, and when the bowl is brought into the warmth, the pot can be removed and another plantpot containing a 'greenery' plant substituted. Ivies or ferns are very attractive with bulbs. The spare pot of bulbs can be used separately or in another plant arrangement.

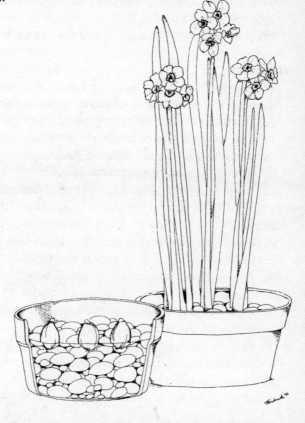

Week One
Bulbs in Water

You need: 1 hyacinth bulb (the larger size, prepared for Christmas flowering)
3 (or more) narcissus bulbs (Paper White, Soleil d'Or)
Hyacinth glass*
Bowl
Pebbles
Water
Pieces of charcoal
Black polythene bag, to use upside down over the hyacinth glass

* You can use a narrow necked pickle jar instead of a special hyacinth glass (try the bulb for size) – or use a 2lb jam jar filled with pebbles or glass marbles on which to rest the bulb.

Hyacinth
1. Fill the hyacinth glass to the neck with water.
2. Add a small piece of charcoal to keep water fresh.
3. Sit the hyacinth bulb firmly in the top of the glass.
4. The base of the bulb should be touching the water so check the level and adjust if necessary.
5. Cover with black polythene bag.
6. Keep in a cool place until the roots start to grow.

Narcissi
1. Put a few pieces of charcoal in the bottom of the bowl.
2. Fill to within 5 cm (2 ins) of the rim with pebbles.
3. Arrange the bulbs. They can be close together, but not touching.
4. Add more pebbles to about half-way up the bulbs; this will hold them firmly in place.
5. Pour in enough water to reach just below the surface of the pebbles, to the base of the bulbs.
6. Place the bowl on the windowsill.

Follow-up

Top up with water when necessary.

When the roots of the hyacinth begin to grow, remove the black bag. Preferably keep the bulb in a fairly cool but light place – a north-facing windowsill for instance – until the flower-spike shows some colour, then bring into a warm room.

Support the narcissi when they grow tall with split canes wedged into the pebbles, and soft string or wool.

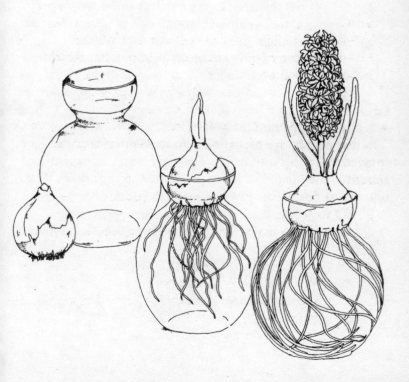

Week Two

Harvesting Ornamental Gourds and Collecting Seed Heads

Harvesting Ornamental Gourds

You need: Ornamental gourds
Secateurs
Water, bowl, nailbrush
Paper towel
Newspaper or a tray

Method:
1. Cut the gourds off the plant with an inch or so of stem left attached to them.
2. The gourds should be washed and scrubbed gently if dirty.
3. Dry them with a paper towel.
4. Set them out to dry on a tray or on newspaper in a well-ventilated room out of direct heat or sunlight.
5. Some fruits will be dry in about a month, others will take longer.

Later

When thoroughly dry, the gourds can be polished with a wax furniture polish, or alternatively painted with clear varnish or sprayed with polyurethane. They are very attractive and colourful piled in a dish or used in flower arrangements. They sell well at fêtes.

Collecting Seedheads

Some seedheads are ready for gathering early and others ripen later in the year. September is the time when most of them are ready for collecting. Some material for drying or preserving will come from the garden – and may even be grown especially for that purpose – and some may be found growing wild. Keeping an eye open for likely material encourages nature-observation on expeditions into the country.

Simple methods of pressing, drying and preserving flowers and leaves have already been given (June Week Five, July Weeks Two, Three and Four), but you may find the following additional hints helpful:

1. Gather seedheads before they are fully ripe – candytuft and nigella can be picked either green or brown.
2. Strip the leaves from the stems before hanging the seedheads in small bunches upside down.
3. Pick physalis (Chinese lanterns) when they turn orange.

Seedheads which scatter seeds. Make muslin bags – or tie on sections of old nylon stockings – to cover the seedheads whilst they are hanging up to dry.

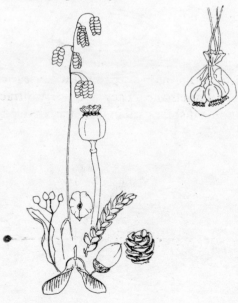

Week Three
Saving Seeds and Collecting Conkers and Acorns

Saving Seeds

Saving Seeds from Your Own Plants
Collect seedheads or pods when they are dry, choosing a warm sunny day. Pick them into paper bags (small seeds cling to plastic) noting the plant they came from. Lay each kind of seedhead in separate box lids or paper-lined trays in a dry place, perhaps a sunny room.

Leave them for a few days and when they are dry gently shake or crush the seedheads to release the seeds. Take peas or beans out of their pods. Separate seeds from the rubbish.

Storing Seeds for Craft Work
Seeds which are clean and dry must be stored in air-tight containers – screwtop glass jars are useful as they enable the contents to be seen at a glance.

Storing Seeds to Grow Next Year

To give seeds the best chance of growing in the following season, it is important to keep them as dry and cool as possible. Pour the seeds into paper envelopes which are properly labelled. Place the envelopes in a screw-top sweet jar together with some silica gel to keep the atmosphere dry. Packets of silica gel often come with newly bought equipment – before using, dry them out thoroughly by placing them over a radiator or in an airing cupboard for an hour or two. Alternatively, silica gel can be bought from a chemist (buy the blue cobalt treated sort – it turns pink when damp and back to blue when dried out). Put a teaspoonful in a small open pot in the storage jar. Leave some space in the jar, do not pack it too lightly, and store in a cool place. Left over packets of bought seeds can be stored in the same way. The vital thing is to avoid warmth and moisture.

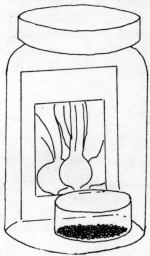

Conkers and Acorns

Horse-chestnuts are fun to collect, and satisfyingly brown and shiny. They can be used in educational topics, for counting and weighing, and so can acorns or beech nuts and seeds from other trees. Small acorns still held firmly in their cups can be used in collage or with dried flowers if they are sprayed or painted with clear varnish to prevent shrivelling.

Fully ripened acorns and 'conkers' will grow into useful patio plants – a pot-grown horse-chestnut can be kept for years without growing tall, and its sticky buds open in spring to give very attractive leaves. Small oak trees can be trained as bonsai and used in miniature gardens.

Chestnuts and acorns (and any other tree seeds) are best planted as soon as possible after collecting, otherwise they shrivel. They will not germinate until they have a spell of cold, so they can either be planted individually in pots in the autumn or stored in damp sand or leaf-mould over the winter and brought indoors to pot up in February or March. Germination is erratic, so the latter method is to be preferred. Sprouting acorns can be grown in a crocus glass or a bottle with a narrow neck, so that the root development can be observed.

You need: A plastic pot with a lid (margarine, cottage cheese, etc.)
Damp sand
Conkers, acorns, etc.
Marker stick or flag

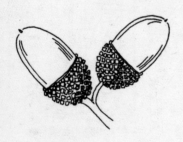

Method: 1. Make holes in the base and lid of the plastic pot.
2. Half-fill the pot with damp sand.
3. Plant 'seeds' close but not touching.
4. Cover with more sand.
5. Put on the lid. This guards against mice and squirrels!
6. Bury in a pile of sand, heap of peat or leafmould, etc.
7. Mark the place – with a label tied to a stick, a flag – or simply remember!

Aftercare
Dig the pot up next year and plant the sprouting seeds.

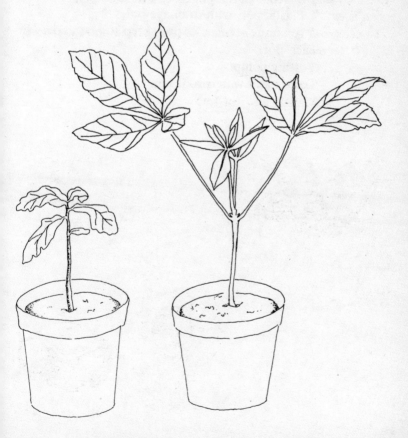

Week Four
A Crocus Adventure

Most varieties of crocus will not flower well if grown indoors –
they like to grow in the cold, and in full light. But they can be
grown outside in pots and brought indoors when the flower
bud is just beginning to show colour. Bringing them into warm
conditions too soon results in all leaves and no flowers. The
purple and purple-striped varieties are the most reliable for
success – but some of the more unusual ones provide an
astonishing display and provoke more excitement and
comment. A few pots of different kinds are well worth the
experiment. Crocus are relatively cheap.

You need: 1 Plastic pot, with drainage holes
              5 (or more) crocus corms (keep to one variety in
              each pot)
              Potting compost
              Labels and waterproof pen

Method:

1. Write the name of the crocus variety on one side of the label and the gardener's name on the other.
2. Fill the pots to 4 cm (1½ ins) from the top and tap the pot to firm the compost.
3. Arrange the corms (taking care to distinguish the base of the corm) and plant them the right way up.
4. Cover the corms with compost. Level off, and tap the pot again. Label.
5. Stand the pots in a 'peat box' outside – a bottomless box with a layer of peat, with more peat round the pots. Alternatively, stand them in a sheltered spot in the garden, half-embedding the pots so that they won't fall over. A piece of fine-meshed wire netting would help to guard against mice and squirrels – both are fond of eating crocus. In the early spring, watch for progress, and bring indoors just before they come into bloom.

Week Five
Making a Terrarium

A terrarium can be made from anything which has transparent sides and has either a restricted neck or an opening which can be covered with a sheet of glass or plastic. The essential thing is that the plants inside are protected from the dry air and draughts which cause so many problems in growing delicate plants. Once planted, very little maintenance is involved. A bottle garden is the most well known form of terrarium but this is very difficult to make, requiring fiddly manoeuvring to get the plants inside. Just as much pleasure can be gained from planting a mini garden in a glass or plastic sweet jar. A goldfish bowl or a fish tank can be used with a transparent covering.

You need: A glass or plastic jar with a lid
Charcoal
Potting compost ready moistened
Small plants
Dibber

Method: 1. Put a layer of charcoal at the bottom of the jar.
2. Add a layer of compost to a quarter of the depth of the jar.
3. 'Landscape' the ground by making a hill or a slope. Make holes with the dibber where you want to place the plants and firm them in.
4. Some clean gravel can be spread on the surface or one or two washed stones or pebbles used to add character, but this is optional.
5. Wipe the sides of the jar clean with a moistened tissue if necessary, then put on the lid.

Aftercare

The terrarium should be placed in good, but indirect light. Never place it in a sunny window.

Plants in a sealed container do not need watering at all – or very rarely – once they are established. For the first week or so, watch for misting, and remove the cover or lid until it has cleared, then seal up again.

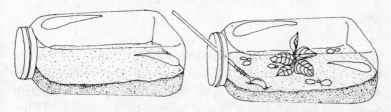

NOTE: Do not use cacti or succulents in a sealed terrarium. Do not use flowering plants – the dead heads would need snipping off. Foliage plants are easier – especially those which do not grow quickly. Choose small plants, that will have room to grow, and pinch them back as they grow.

Suitable Plants

Small-leafed ivy
Ferns
Fittonia (snakeskin plant)
Ficus pumila (creeping fig)

Peperomia
Pilea (aluminium plant)
Saxifraga sarmentosa
(mother of thousands)

October

Week One
Autumn Tidy – Hanging Baskets and Containers

Tidying up the garden makes it look less forlorn in the winter. Hanging baskets need to be taken down and outdoor containers made ready for planting with spring flowers. Some of the plants can be put into pots and kept indoors over the winter, ready to use again next year. Annuals such as petunias and marigolds will be at the end of their useful life and should be thrown away.

Some perennials, such as golden thyme or aubretia, can be planted elsewhere in the garden or replanted in the container to grow with the next lot of plants. They can be replanted immediately, or dug out with plenty of soil around them and put into a box or big pot to wait until you are ready for the 'spring planting' session (October Week Three). Permanent plants such as conifers should, of course, not be disturbed.

You need: Big plastic sheet
Trowel
Plant pots, for the plants to be saved
Drainage material if required
Secateurs or scissors

Method: 1. Be ruthless – tip out the hanging basket onto the plastic sheet and sort out the plants to be thrown away. Keep the roots of the ones which are to be saved as undisturbed as possible.

When dealing with a container, dig in with the trowel and get the plants out onto the plastic sheet for sorting. Discard the annuals and any sad-looking or diseased plants.

2. Put some drainage material into the bottom of each plant pot (but not if they are to stand on capillary matting). A little fresh compost is good, but not absolutely necessary.

3. Trim off the dead leaves and flowers and pot up the plants. If the roots are too big to fit in the pot, snip some of them off.

4. Water and drain. Let them settle for a few days in good light but not hot sun before putting in their winter place, perhaps on a sunny windowsill.

Plants to keep

Fuchsias	Begonias – fibrous rooted
Geraniums	(semperflorens)
Begonias – tuberous	

All of these plants are tender and need to be kept in a frost free place over the winter:

Fuchsias: Gradually reduce the water and keep the compost barely moist over the winter. Store in a frost-free, rather cool place. The plants will become dormant and drop their leaves so they do not need much light.

Geraniums: Geraniums need as much light as possible in the winter. In a warm room, they will go on flowering, but in a cool room keep them rather dry.

Begonias: Tuberous begonias should be lifted and put in a dry place to shrivel. After drying the tubers on a sunny windowsill, store them in a frost-free place until starting into growth again in March. Fibrous begonias can be potted up and kept on a windowsill to flower all winter.

Lobelia: Lobelia also makes a potted plant to keep on a windowsill in the winter.

Week Two
Dried Flower Arranging

A selection of dried plant material might include:
>   Everlasting flowers (Acrolinium, Statice, Helichrysum, Achillea)
>   Globe thistle (Echinops)
>   Ornamental grasses, seedheads (Poppy, Allium, etc.)
>   Dried or glycerined leaves or ferns

A Very Simple Dried Flower Arrangement

You need: A selection of dried plant material
>   Vase, jar or tin covered with decorative paper
>   Clean dry sand

Method: 1. Fill the container with sand to about 2.5 cm (1 in) below the rim.
>   2. Arrange the flowers and other dry material, breaking or cutting the stems as necessary.

A Flower Arrangement in Oasis

Special dried-flower Oasis can be bought in small blocks with sticky pads attached. Alternatively, you can cut small blocks and fix them to the container with a kind of very sticky putty, Oasis-Fix, sold in the same shops where you buy the Oasis. You can also use ordinary Oasis dry. As there is no water to be used, dried flowers can be used on any kind of base and do not necessarily need a container. Obliquely cut slices of logs, smoothed and varnished but retaining the bark, are very attractive. Shallow pottery dishes, wicker baskets and straw mats are other possibilities.

You need: A base or container
>   Oasis (dry)
>   Oasis-fix
>   Scissors or secateurs if needed

Method: 1. Fix the Oasis to the base or container.
2. Arrange the long spiky material first.
3. Place the largest material towards the centre and base of the arrangement.
4. Fill in with the rest of the material.
5. Check that the Oasis is hidden. If not, add some leaves.

NOTE: For basic flower arranging see June Week Three.

Week Three
Planting for Spring

Now is the time to prepare a hanging basket for the spring.

You need: A hanging basket
Plastic lining with drainage holes
Potting compost, ready moistened
A few pieces of charcoal (optional)
Bulbs – short-stemmed tulips (3 or more), dwarf narcissi or grape hyacinths, or a mixture of all three
Primula plants (3 or 4)
Aubretia plants (3 or 4)

Method:
1. To prepare the hanging basket, see May Week Three notes.
2. Group the tulip bulbs in the middle of the basket, covering them with 5–8 cm (2–3 ins) of compost.
3. Space the primulas around them and plant aubretias round the edge of the basket.
4. Water sparingly.
5. Stand on a sand or gravel tray in a cool greenhouse, in a cold frame, or bed in sand in a sheltered place in the garden.

Aftercare
Check occasionally to see whether watering is needed, and when the bulbs begin to grow make sure that the basket is in full light. Hang up in the spring.

Alternative
Plant an outdoor container instead of a basket. Use variegated ivies instead of aubretia. Choose different bulbs: iris reticulata, crocus, roman hyacinths, etc., with pansies. Myosotis (forget-me-nots) mix well with tulips or wallflowers, and in a larger container a dwarf conifer in the centre will add contrast.

Week Four

A Collage Picture

You need: A selection of dried or preserved plant material such as:

        Dried flowers (Helichrysum, Acroclinium, Statice, etc.)

        Dried seedheads

        Larch cones

        Grasses

        Pressed leaves

        Seeds and pieces of bark

Two pieces of card 20 cm × 25 cm (8 ins × 10 ins) approximately, coloured or covered with textured wallpaper

UHU glue – or any transparent glue

Scissors

Tweezers for handling small plant material

Braid edging and tape loop

Method:

A. Preparing the background:

   1. Cut the wallpaper to the same size as the card.

   2. Paste the card and press the paper on it.

   3. Let it dry.

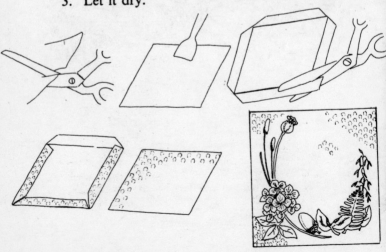

NOTE: A neater finish is obtained by cutting the paper 5 cm (2 ins) larger than the card all round, and sticking over the back, cutting off the corners of the paper to get a neater fit (see diagram).

Papers with a 'canvas' or 'slubbed silk' weave, or a natural look, like 'cork' or 'grass matting' look most attractive.

B. Making the picture:
1. Lay out the design on the first piece of card. This makes it easier to experiment, and to transfer the pieces, gluing them down in their final positions on the second piece of card.
2. Lay out the main features of the design first.
3. Add leaves and smaller features to make a satisfying picture.
4. Transfer the material to the second piece of card, and glue it on. Use the glue sparingly and remember to glue down the back leaves first.
5. The picture can be finished with neat braid glued round the edge, and a tape loop glued to the back for hanging.

Alternatives:
The picture can be made in a shoe box lid, or on a straw mat instead.

November

Hanging Stars

Many wild and garden flowers produce attractive seed heads and there are all kinds of natural materials such as dried grasses, cones and seeds which can be used in decorations like these. Trying out variations stimulates the imagination, and this is a session which can be repeated with enjoyment.

Collecting material adds point to autumn outings and may spark off an interest in botany. Before the next session some things can be sprayed or painted. Cow parsley, like fennel, looks very good sprayed in white, and larch cones make attractive centres in red or orange. For Christmas, the stars can be sprayed in gold or silver and hung on the tree.

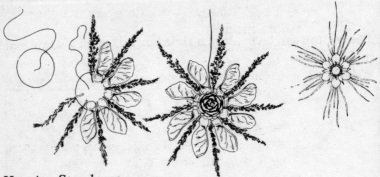

Hanging Star 1.
You need: For each decoration:
   A 2.5 cm (1 in) diameter disc of card (coloured if possible)
   A piece of strong thread (button or linen thread) about 30 cm (12 ins) long
   Quick-drying adhesive (UHU or Bostick no 1)
   Dried grasses, seedheads, etc.

Suitable dried material

For the 'star': dried grasses, oats, long pine needles, ash and sycamore seeds, bits of cow-parsley seed heads.

For the centres: dried flowers, larch cones, poppy heads, small teasels, etc., or seeds.

Method:
1. Glue one end of the thread onto the card (the card can be held down on the work table with a blob of plasticine or Blu-tack if there are problems in holding it steady)
2. Glue on the 'star' material.
3. Attach the chosen centre flower or cone with a dab of glue, or brush the centre with glue and sprinkle with seeds, such as lentils.
4. Leave to dry.
5. Hang up – a number of these together will make an attractive mobile.

Hanging Star 2.

You need: A small lump of plasticine the size of a hazel nut 30 cm (12 in) piece of strong thread (linen or button thread)
Dried grasses, seeds, flowers, etc.

Method:
1. Soften the plasticine. Break it in half and roll into two balls.
2. Flatten one ball into a disc, pressed to the work surface.
3. Tie the ends of the thread together and press the knot onto the disc.
4. Arrange grasses, pine needles, etc., to radiate from the disc, pressing the ends onto the plasticine.
5. Place the other ball of plasticine on top and flatten, to cover and hold the ends of the grasses.
6. Press a dried flower or a few seeds into the centre. (The other side can be decorated too, if desired.) Hang by the loop of thread.

Week Two
A Succulent Dish Garden

Succulents are ideal plants for the dry atmosphere produced by central heating, and a dish garden like this needs very little attention. A dish or seed-tray 7–8 cm (3 ins) deep, a plastic or pottery bowl or a shallow tureen would be best. Succulent gardens last a long time, so a temporary container such as a foil dish would be inappropriate. If the container does not have holes, provide some pebbles or charcoal for drainage. Succulents do not need much nourishment, so a peat-based seed compost can be used, or potting compost mixed with an equal quantity of coarse sand, or a special succulent mix.

You need: A container, with drainage material if necessary
Compost (as above)
Water
Succulent plants or rooted succulent cuttings (see August Week Three)
Stones, gravel, sand, coloured chippings, etc.

Method: 1. Moisten and mix the compost.
2. Fill the container to within 2 cm (¾ in) of the rim.
3. Arrange the plants so that they make an interesting 'landscape', tall ones in the middle, low ones at the edge.
4. Arrange stones, scatter the surface of the compost between the plants with sand, gravel, or chippings.

NOTE: Children may like to add toy figures or animals to the landscape.

Aftercare
Place in a south-facing windowsill, or in a bright spot. The harder-leaved succulents like most sun. Very little water is needed in winter.

Suitable Plants

As stated in August Week Three, it is best to avoid those succulents, such as agave or aloe, that have vicious spines on their leaves. Those listed below come in many fascinating varieties that will provide interesting combinations of colour and shape when grown together.

Bryophyllum (Good Luck Plant)
Crassula argentea (Jade Plant)
Echeveria
Sedum
Sempervivum (Houseleek, etc.)
Senecio (String of Beads Plant)
Kalanchoë

Week Three
A Pressed Flower Picture

Pressed flowers and leaves make very pretty pictures and often the simplest designs are the most effective. The material can be arranged in a natural design such as a spray, or in a geometrical pattern, or as a fun-picture, to depict animals, birds or fish. Dark backgrounds show the pressed flowers to best advantage.

A certain amount of manual dexterity is required, and the secret of success is to use only very tiny dabs of glue. A toothpick or the pointed handle of a paintbrush, as suggested below, will pick up just enough, either from a tube or from a small amount of glue in a tin lid. Transparent glue is preferable – but a rubber-based one may allow more time for positioning the flowers.

The materials are delicate and need protection from dust and damp air, so the pictures must be covered in some way. A first effort could be sprayed with several coats of transparent plastic varnish. A ready-made frame with glass or plastic could be used – but not a slide-in photograph frame. Look out for odd frames at jumble-sales. Another possibility is to use a sheet of glass or rigid transparent plastic. Sticky plastic tape (or passe-partout) round the edges will hold it and the cardboard backing together. This, however, needs skilful handling.

When the picture is hung, it should be placed out of direct sunlight to prevent the colours fading quickly.

Making Your Picture

You need: Small picture frame with glass
Pressed flowers and leaves (see June Week Five)
Cardboard, coloured, to fit the frame
A piece of paper the same size for practice
A small paintbrush
Transparent glue

Method:

1. Lay out a selection of dried flowers and leaves on the practice paper.
2. Avoid too much handling – use a small paintbrush to move them around and make a design that you like.
3. Use leaves at the base of the design to give 'weight' and use delicate material at the top and edges. Raspberry leaves can be used on their grey side.
4. Using the brush handle, gently dab spots of adhesive onto the flowers, and transfer them to the coloured card. Remember – things that go at the back of the design should be stuck on first.
5. When the picture is complete, press the glass down over it and leave to dry.
6. Fix into the frame.

Alternatives

Bookmarks and birthday cards can be made, using clear plastic adhesive film to cover them. This is rather tricky to smooth evenly over the picture, so experiment first.

Week Four
A Seed Mosaic

Designs of seeds glued to thick cardboard or hardboard can be either simple or complicated. The seeds are chosen to provide different colours and textures, and it is possible to choose a variety of large seeds which will be easy to handle. Dried beans, peas, lentils and cereals can be bought in supermarkets, grocers' or health food shops. Melon and marrow seeds can be rescued from the kitchen bin and washed and spread out to dry on paper. You can do the same with cherry stones and fruit pips, and there are many other nuts and seeds which can be collected on country walks or from the garden. For safety, do not use any seeds which are poisonous (see Poisonous Plants, page 204).

Coloured card is less intimidating than white, and will look more attractive in the spaces between the seeds. Hardboard is a good colour – use the rough side – both texture and colour suiting the natural 'earthy' look of the seeds. Handling seeds in

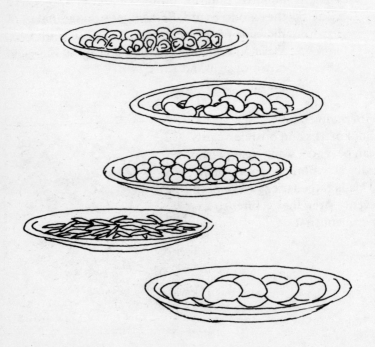

this activity gives practice in hand/eye co-ordination, and provides opportunities to discuss colour, texture, shape and size. A square shape is easiest to start with.

You need: A piece of thick card or hardboard, 20 cm × 20 cm (8 ins × 8 ins)
Glue and a stick or spatula, or a glue pen
15 cm (6 ins) of ribbon or tape
Pencil or piece of charcoal
A selection of dried seeds such as:
Beans (many sizes and colours – from butter beans to mung beans)
Lentils and peas (whole and split)
Wheat, barley, rice, maize
Beechnuts, sycamore, ash seeds
Sunflower, nasturtium, melon seeds

Method for Large Seeds

1. Put out the seeds in lids or saucers for easy access.
2. Glue the seeds one by one in a pattern on the card or hardboard, using a dab of adhesive. A simple 'starter' is a sunburst design, radiating outwards from the centre.

Alternatively, a geometrical pattern working from the corners inwards. This is the reason for choosing a square-shaped background for the first effort.

3. Leave to dry.

Method for Small Seeds

1. Draw a rough design in pencil or charcoal on the base card.
2. Using adhesive on a spatula, or a glue pen, draw in one of the lines or fill in a small area of the design.
3. Sprinkle the card with the required seed, then pick up the base card and gently shake off over a clean piece of paper. The seed will stick to the glued areas and not to the rest.
4. Pour the unused seed back into the jar, or save separately for a later part of the design (A warning here against mixed up seeds!)
5. Repeat with various seeds as required for the rest of the design. Large seeds can be added individually.
6. Leave to dry.

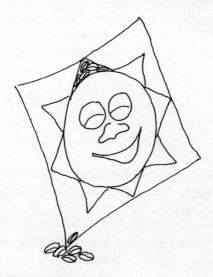

Hanging the Seed-Mosaic Picture

Unless you have used a fast-drying glue, you may have to wait until the following week to fix the tape or ribbon hangers, to avoid disturbing the design.

1. Cut the tape (or ribbon) into 2 equal pieces.
2. Fold each in half.
3. Glue to the back of the picture at the top corners. This gives a stronger support than a single hanger, and less likelihood of the picture hanging crookedly.

December

Week One
Making a 'Poinsettia' Plant

This is an inexpensive and effective decoration which looks like a growing plant. The ivy stays fresh for several weeks if the sand is kept damp.

You need: For the plant   Sprays of ivy with leaves and berries
Red crêpe paper for petals
Fine wire – fuse wire or the sort used by florists

For the
container   A clean, empty tin
Damp sand
Patterned paper
Sellotape or glue
Scissors

Method: First decorate the tin:
1. Cut a strip of paper the depth of the tin.
2. Roll the paper round the tin.
3. Glue or sellotape the end.
4. Fill the tin with damp sand.

Now make the plant:

1. Cut red crêpe paper into rectangles 8 cm × 20 cm (3½ ins × 8 ins).
2. Fold the strips of paper into halves, quarters and then eighths – or zig-zag as in the diagram.
3. Cut these into petal shapes (see diagram).
4. Bunch the paper round the ivy berries and wind round it with fine wire, arranging the petals to make a flower round the ivy berry centre.
5. Make each cluster of ivy berries into a flower in the same way.
6. Arrange the sprays of ivy in the pot, pushing the ends firmly into the damp sand.

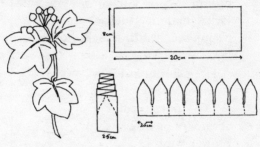

Alternatives

1. Wire or glue flowers (paper or dried) to twigs.
2. Fix dried flowers into an Oasis cone with pins or hairpins.
3. Make a 'tree' by sticking short sprigs of evergreens into an Oasis cone. Small larch cones on wires, ribbon bows or Christmas baubles may be added.

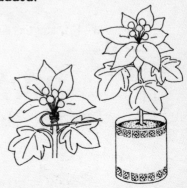

Week Two

Christmas Decorations (1) – Spraying Gold

Leaves, cones and dried materials are often more effective in decorations for Christmas if they have been sprayed gold, silver, white or scarlet. Since they need to dry thoroughly before being used, it is a good idea to prepare them the week before. This also gives an opportunity to discuss plans for decorations, collect other things such as tinsel, ribbons, and baubles, and to become familiar with the plant material.

You need: Evergreens, such as holly, butcher's broom
Dried material such as fir cones, poppy seedheads, teasels, honesty, larch twigs, etc.
A large cardboard box
A can of spray
A large potato cut in half
Secateurs or flower snips
Flower wires

} For two to four people

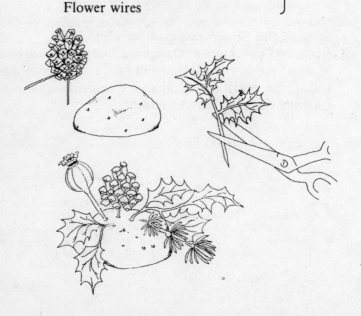

Method: 1. Prepare the cones by twisting one end of a piece of flower wire round the 'petals' at the base of the cone.
2. Place the potato cut side down on the table.
3. Shorten the stems of the plant material and remove any unattractive or untidy bits that will not be effective when sprayed.
4. Push the wired cones and the plant stems into the potato.
5. With the open end of the box facing, stand the potato inside it. Shake the spray well, then holding the can at arm's length, spray the material in the box. Beware of over-enthusiasm! Leave for a few minutes, then turn the potato round and spray the other side of the 'arrangement'.
6. Wait a few minutes, then remove from the box and leave to dry.

Variations
1. With a co-operative effort, all the cones can be sprayed one colour and leaves another.
2. Jars of sand can be used instead of the potato, if pushing in the stems proves difficult.

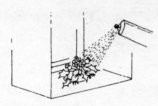

Week Three
Christmas Decorations (2) –
A Christmas Log

You need: A half log
Two nails and a hammer
Small block of Oasis
Cones – wired and sprayed
Sprigs of evergreen, sprayed leaves, etc.
Ribbon ⎫
Plastic baubles ⎬ Optional
A strong hairpin ⎭

Method: 1. Hammer two nails into the log. (This can be prepared beforehand)
2. Push the block of Oasis foam onto the nails.
3. Arrange green or sprayed plant material by pushing stems into the Oasis.
4. Add the cones.
5. Make a ribbon bow, and fix it (or the baubles) in the Oasis with the hairpin.

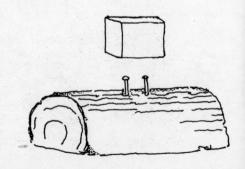

Week Four
Peanuts for the Birds

Feeding the Birds
Winter is a bad time for the birds and it is easy to attract them nearer to the house by putting out food and water. A bird table, or a bird feeder hanging on a tree or post where it can be seen from a window, will provide hours of pleasure. A good place to hang a feeder is on the bracket used for hanging baskets in the summer. A feeder fixed just outside a window and food sprinkled on a windowsill will attract tits and robins for very close observation. Feeding the birds regularly and keeping it up throughout the winter will encourage them to make a habit of visiting the garden.

Providing a variety of foods will attract different kinds of birds. Greenfinches and chaffinches are seed eaters – they love wheat and oats as well as the seed of wild grasses. Thrushes, blackbirds and robins enjoy scraps of fat, cooked potato, bits of apple and a few sultanas as well as breadcrumbs. Tits love nuts and seeds. Hang up a sunflower seed head or make a peanut string.

NOTE: Do not feed the birds in the spring and summer as this kind of food is not suitable for taking back to the nest and may choke baby birds.

Peanuts
Try to buy peanuts still in their shells – the ones which haven't been roasted. They can be bought in a greengrocer's or a pet shop. If you cannot find peanuts in shells buy the raw shelled ones (not salted) in a supermarket or natural food shop. A plastic net bag can be filled with shelled peanuts to make a feeder for the birds instead of making the peanut string suggested opposite.

Make a Peanut String for the Birds

Version A
You need: Peanuts in their shells
              A piece of string 60–100 cm (2–3 ft) long

Method: 1. Loop the end of the string round the first peanut
                 and tie a knot.
              2. Continue to tie in peanuts all the way up the
                 string almost to the end. Make a loop for
                 hanging up.

Version B
You need: Peanuts in their shells
              Darning or tapestry needle
              Strong thread

Method: 1. Thread the needle. Make a
                 big knot at the end of the
                 thread or tie it round the
                 first peanut.
              2. Thread the rest of the pea-
                 nuts on to the string. Tie a
                 loop for hanging.

Additional Suggestions
1. Examine a peanut, split it and look inside. You will be
   able to see the embryo plant in the centre.
2. Plant a few of the nuts about 2.5 cm (1 in) deep in moist
   seed compost in a pot and put the pot in a plastic bag.
   Germinate in a warm place (e.g. shelf above a radiator)
   for two to three weeks. Once sprouted, keep as warm as
   possible and in full light. Peanuts like sunshine and plenty
   of water.

NOTE: The peanut is not a nut but the seed of an annual which
is related to the pea family.

Appendices

1 About Horticultural Therapy

The Society for Horticultural Therapy (HT) is the UK national charity set up in 1978 to provide advice, information and support to elderly and disabled gardeners and those who work with them.

HT helps by:

- *Training* — occupational therapists and others using horticulture in their work with people with all kinds of disadvantages, so that they feel confident in their skills to lead others in gardening activities and to develop successful therapy programmes.
- *Project Advice* — for those about to set up horticultural projects to benefit people in care settings, so that they can be sure of the best chance of horticultural and therapeutic success.
- *Land Use Volunteer Service* — which enables skilled young horticulturalists to use their energy and expertise to get projects started and learn about working with people at the same time.
- *Growth Point* — the magazine which keeps people and projects in touch with new developments, interesting ideas and solutions to common problems, and which tries to relieve the isolation felt by many carers and disabled or elderly people.
- *Demonstration Gardens* — local bases for groups and individuals to get encouragement in gardening, try out facilities and see ideas in action.
- *Advice and Workshop Service* — answering thousands of queries a year from individuals with simple or serious problems with their gardening; offering practical demonstrations around the country.
- *Advisory Committee for Blind Gardeners* — responds to requests for information and organises practical gardening weekends and seminars for visually impaired people and those who work with them.

Membership of HT means that you
- receive *Growth Point*, HT's quarterly magazine, free
- get help with your gardening problems
- hear from others, and swap ideas, plants, recipes, seeds
- buy tools, aids, sundries and publications at a reduced cost
- hear about workshops and study days first
- use HT's library and information services
- advertise free in *Growth Point*
- meet others at HT's Annual Meeting
- help other gardeners with special needs.

You can find out more from:
Horticultural Therapy, Goulds Ground, Vallis Way, Frome, Somerset BA11 3DW. Tel: (0373) 64782

2 Publications of Special Relevance to Gardening with Disabled and Disadvantaged People

Available from HT

HT 'Bookshop'. A catalogue of more than eighty information leaflets on a range of topics for disabled and handicapped gardeners and those who work with them. Available free on request.

Growth Point. The quarterly magazine for gardeners with special needs and those who work with them. Free to members of HT, or on subscription to non-members (details on request).

Library Facilities. HT has a unique collection of published and unpublished material relating to horticulture and gardening for disabled and disadvantaged people. Details of the facilities and their uses are contained in *HT 'Bookshop'*.

Able to Garden, edited by Peter Please. Batsford Books, 1990. Also available from bookshops.

A book version of HT's information leaflets providing practical advice and ideas for people with disabilities and those who work with them.

Available from the Federation to Promote Horticulture for Disabled People

A selection of publications on therapeutic horticulture. Details available from John Catlin, 252 The Ridgeway, Enfield, Middlesex EN2 8AP.

Other Publications

City Farmer. The quarterly magazine for Community Gardens and City Farms. Published by the National Federation of City Farms Ltd., The Old Vicarage, 66 Fraser

Street, Windmill Hill, Bedminster, Bristol BS3 4LY. Tel: (0272) 660663. (Details of annual subscription and single issue prices available on request.)

Contains news, views, ideas, advice and information on City Farms and Community Gardens. Also lists all member Gardens and Farms.

City Farming and Community Gardening by Christopher Wardle, edited by Kay Knights. InterChange Books, 1983. Available from bookshops or from InterChange, 15 Wilkins Street, London NW5 3NG. Tel: 071-267 9421.

Comprehensive information on how to set up and run a neighbourhood City Farm and Community Garden in Britain.

Gardening and the Handicapped Child by Patricia Elliot. Disabled Living Foundation, 1978. Available from Haigh & Hochland, The Precinct Centre, Oxford Road, Manchester M13 9QA. Tel: 061-273 4156.

Inspiration for teachers and instructors — full of ideas. Practical and educational aspects, hobbies, further education, employment. Useful appendices: bibliography, addresses, suppliers.

Gardening in Retirement by Alec Bristow. RHS Wisley Handbook. Available from RHS Enterprises, Wisley Gardens, Woking, Surrey GU23 6QB. Tel: (0483) 211113.

An overview on gardening in later years. Contains many useful tips, ideas and advice on design, etc.

Gardening in Retirement by Isobel Pays. Age Concern. Available from bookshops or from Age Concern, 60 Pitcairn Road, Mitcham, Surrey CR4 3LL. Tel: 081-640 5432.

Contains ideas for adapting an existing garden for more efficient maintenance and for increased enjoyment as you have more time to spend. Foreword by Dame Vera Lynn and an introduction by Percy Thrower.

Gardening Without Sight by Kathleen Fleet. Royal National Institute for the Blind. Available free from RNIB, 224

Portland Street, London W1N 6AA. Tel: 071-388 1266.

Gardening books in Braille are available on loan from National Library for the Blind, Cromwell Road, Bradbury, Stockport, Cheshire.

Come Gardening and the *Cassette Library for Blind Gardeners*. Cassettes loaned on payment of an annual subscription. Miss Kathleen Fleet, 48 Tolcarne Drive, Pinner, Middlesex HA5 2DQ.

Come Gardening (formerly *The Gardener*)is a quarterly magazine for visually impaired gardeners. Produced on cassette tape and in Braille, it comprises articles, news, ideas, gardening queries and product information. Subscription also covers the Cassette Library with its wide range of gardening subjects.

Keep on Growing by Susan Hale. Herefordshire DIAL, 1985. Available from Herefordshire DIAL, 15 St Owen Street, Hereford HR1 2JB. Tel: (0432) 277770.

A Herefordshire guide for disabled and elderly gardeners. Tips and techniques, local nurseries, garden centres, stockists and gardens to visit in Hereford and Worcester.

Gardening, compiled by D. Hollinrake. Edited by G.M. Cochrane and E.R. Wilshere. Equipment for the Disabled, 1987. Available from Equipment for the Disabled (Dept EU), Mary Marlborough Lodge, Nuffield Orthopaedic Centre, Headington, Oxford OX3 7LD. Tel: (0865) 750103.

Invaluable and comprehensive information on garden design, plants, tools, safety, propagation, resources, bibliography, clubs for disabled gardeners, etc.

Therapeutic Horticulture by Rosemary Hagedorn. Winslow Press, 1987. Available from bookshops.

Aimed primarily at Occupational Therapists, contains lots of useful information on special designs, therapeutic analysis, task content, programming, safety, techniques, etc. Also includes an invaluable list of references and sources of information.

Out of Doors with Handicapped People by Mike Cotton. Human Horizons Series, Souvenir Press, 1981. Available from bookshops.

Intended for use by handicapped young people themselves, by their parents and teachers. An illustrated guide to the environment of towns, parks and gardens, woodlands, farms, seashore and moors and mountains. Contains many practical ideas for activities.

3 Other Organisations, Tools and Materials

Organisations

Gardens for the Disabled Trust, Church Cottage, Headcorn, Kent TN27 9NP. Provides support to disabled gardeners in the form of grants.

Provides support to disabled gardeners in the form of grants. Also operates the Garden Club and provides gardening advice.

Tools and Materials

Tools, materials and sundries are constantly changing with new products being brought on to the market. For up to the minute information on manufacturers and suppliers contact Horticultural Therapy, Goulds Ground, Vallis Way, Frome, Somerset BA11 3DW. Tel: (0373) 64782.

4 Poisonous Plants

There are some plants which are poisonous and could actually cause death, and others which may cause pain and vomiting, trigger off an attack of asthma, or by contact with the skin, cause irritation or a rash. Sometimes it is only part of the plant which has this toxic effect, the leaves of rhubarb, for instance.

It is a responsibility to see that plants of this sort are excluded from a programme where there is any possibility of them causing harm. Children, of course, are especially vulnerable, but so are people who have become vague and forgetful through age or brain-damage, and those who are mentally handicapped. Some people are especially sensitive and are allergic to plants which are quite harmless to other people, so one must also be alert for any sign of discomfort.

---

1. Wild Arum (Cuckoo Pint, Lords and Ladies). The cluster of red berries, if handled, can cause dermatitis; if eaten, can cause burning of mouth and irritation of stomach with severe diarrhoea.

2. Yew (Taxus baccata). The pink berries are very poisonous and can cause death from heart failure in a few minutes.

3. Laburnum tree. The commonest cause of plant poisoning in Britain. Its seeds – which look like 'dolly's pea pods' – are attractive to children, but if eaten can kill.

4. Verdigris Agaric (Stropharia aeruginosa). Distinctive blue-green cap which discolours to yellowish brown when older. Found in woods, often under pines, August to November. Fairly poisonous and in susceptible people will cause severe gastric disorders.

5. Deadly Nightshade (Atropa belladonna). Sometimes grows on wasteground or as a garden weed. The berries have been mistaken for black cherries; only two or three can kill a child.

6. Death Cap (Amanita phalloides). Cap is variable in colour but basically greenish tan. Found in woody areas, particularly near oaks and often in bracken, August to November. Intensely poisonous and almost always results in death if eaten.

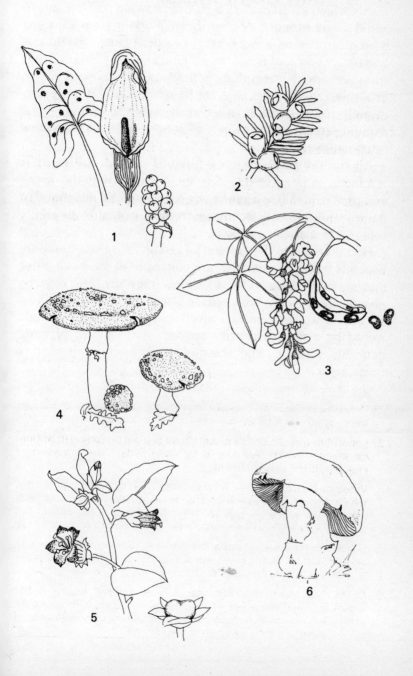

You need a good source of information and pictures of the plants which are named. It is no use knowing which plants to avoid if you cannot recognise them! Working from a list you need illustrated reference books of garden plants, wild flowers and fungi. You could send for posters, or make posters of your own, perhaps photographing or drawing the poisonous plants, or displaying examples on a nature table. Again, it is a matter of judgement, deciding whether it is better to take quiet avoiding action on the subject of poisonous plants or to draw attention to them.

All kinds of plants may be poisonous – wild or cultivated. It is a factor to be taken into account when choosing the shrubs and trees in planning a garden, or collecting wild material on a nature walk, as well as buying an indoor plant or picking a topic for a gardening session.

One must judge the amount of risk in any given situation. Daffodil bulbs, for instance, are poisonous to eat, but it is not dangerous to handle them. Unless they are likely to be mistaken for onions, or there is a real risk that they will be chewed, it would seem excessively cautious to avoid them. It would be a pity to deprive anyone of the joy of planting daffodils when a little sensible supervision is all that is necessary.

5 Butterflies in Your Garden

Choosing plants which are attractive to butterflies encourages them to visit the garden and provides opportunities to observe them closely. Here are some of the flowers that butterflies like:

Alyssum
Aster
Aubretia
Buddleia
Cornflower
Echium
Heliotrope
Honesty
Lavender
Michaelmas Daisy

Mignonette
Phlox
Polyanthus
Sweet Rocket
Sweet William
Sedum Spectabile
Thrift
Valerian
Verbena
Wallflower